A TRANSFORMED HEART

Grief's Healing Journey

Heart to Heart Spiritual Care

CLARE BIEDENHARN, DMIN, BCC

Your Listening Partner, LLC

Contents

Introduction vii

Part I
I Trusted the Voice and I Trust It Still
The Past

Coffee: the Elixir of Love or How It All Began	3
Gratitude	7
Empty Monuments	11

Part II
Grief is More Than a Thing
Grieving

Stone of Grief	17
Salty Venice	27
Stone and Kin	31
Bandwidth and Scarcity	35

Part III
When I Became a Butterfly
Transformation

Cocoon	43
Fall Colors	47
Steps of Change	51
Silent Growth	55

Part IV
Coming Back to Center
Mental Well-being

What Is Your Worst Nightmare	61
Trolls	65
Reluctant Vision	69
Bridging the Gap	73
Umbrellas of Wellbeing	81

Part V
Heart to Heart: The Journey to Deep Listening
Listening

Mountains of Expectations	87
Deep Listening	93
Crumbs	95
Stray Friends	99
Trilobite	103

Part VI
Taking the Plunge
Action

Grounding 5, 4, 3, 2, 1	109
Timeline	113
Ancestor Trees	117
Rebuilding After COVID	121
Bolero	125

Part VII
It Takes a Village
Community

Mirror Talk	133
Secret Code	137
Being Number One	141
Special Love	145
Airport Realizations	151

Part VIII
Going Forward Despite Myself
Growth

Liminal Space	157
The Holly Tree	161
Pass the Baton	167
Emerging From the Hermitage	173

Part IX
Put It Under a Bushel? NO!
Light

Good Vibrations	179
Spokes On a Wheel	183
This Little Light of Mine	187

Part X
Fruition
Closure

View From the Back Seat	193
I Thought I Knew	197
About the Author	201
Also by Clare Biedenharn, DMin, BCC	205
Bibliography	207

Copyright © MMXXIV by Your Listening Partner, LLC

All rights reserved. This book or any portion thereof may not be reproduced or used in any manner whatsoever without the express written permission of the publisher except for the use of brief quotations in a book review.

Printed in the United States of America

First Printing, 2024

ISBN: 979-8-9912630-0-9

ISBN: 979-8-9912630-1-6

Library of Congress Control Number: 2024915990

Independently published by Your Listening Partner, LLC

Introduction
FROM THE AUTHOR

The first time at any new gym can be awkward. That's the way I felt at my initial early morning exercise class as I stepped into the YMCA swimming pool. The water was cold but the welcome I received was warm even at 7:00 am on a chilly morning.

This particular class worked well because I could exercise and then be home to cook my sick husband's breakfast just as he was waking up. I chose this water exercise class for convenience not knowing what a lifeline this welcoming place would provide.

It was only after my husband's death that our son shared James' concern about this new life of widowhood that I was stepping into. James knew me well and that included the part of me that might enjoy aloneness a little too much. In response to his father's fears our son made me promise that I would speak to one human every day.

Once he was gone and I was alone, this time of YMCA community gave me the opportunity to fulfill that promise. Upon James' death the members of my exercise class embraced me and held me accountable. If I didn't show up for a few days, they came to find me. When I shared with them the latest writing project, they cheered me on.

Introduction

I began blogging on my website, https://YourListeningPartner.com, after I published my first book, *Heart to Heart: Spiritual Care through Deep Listening.*

Writing has long been a comfort to me and too soon I began sketching out a memoir. In my heart, though, I knew I wasn't ready. I was still processing my grief. I began instead with small essays and monthly blogs.

My energy shifted with the essay "From the Backseat." First my best friend Karen, told me I was ready to write my story. Then members of my water exercise class told me I was ready. In fact, the class told me I was more than ready. With something like divine intervention this book came together as most of the class, including Bob, our 95-year old, gathered in the Y's meeting room to participate in something of a flashmob of words and finger food rather than music. They had read the blogs and with their added insight we pulled together a map to invite the reader to come along with me on the journey.

Ideas and exercises about working with grief appear in my second book, "Reflect, Reconnect, Restore: Healing from Secondary Grief." The essays in this book are not specific to my transformation through grief, but as I reread them, I realized how grief permeated every aspect of my life especially my writing.

If you are looking for entertainment, welcome. If you are looking for solace, welcome. May these words you read embrace you and bring you comfort on your own journey toward healing at whatever point you may be.

Clare

Introduction

Ordering Information:

Special discounts are available on quantity purchases by coprporations, associations, and others who purchase directly from the author. Contact drclare@yourlisteningpartner.com for details.

PART I

I Trusted the Voice and I Trust It Still
THE PAST

Coffee: the Elixir of Love or How It All Began

WHO COULD HAVE GUESSED that not finding a parking place could be a life changer?

The Camellia Grill, a neighborhood coffee shop, was my third choice as a place to catch a quick bite of supper and it was the only one with a nearby parking space on the packed New Orleans streets.

I was a buyer trainee at the old Maison Blanche department store on Canal St and my $90 a week salary required a tight budget. The old phlegm green 1972 Chevy Nova was my parents' gift to start me on the young adult path of life. I was in the buyer training program and the next day was our final exam. I was planning to grab a bite to eat and go home to review for the test.

Camellia Grill only offered counter service, so I was glad it wasn't as crowded as usual. The cheapest thing on the menu was vegetable soup so I ordered that with extra crackers. Water was my beverage of choice.

That night my life took a new direction as a tall, good-looking young man walked through the door and scanned around for an empty stool. If I'd been a hunter dog, I could have won a champion prize for my 'on point' as I watched him move in my direction. He didn't sit next to me but sat one stool over and ordered coffee. He was incredibly handsome.

And then it happened. I heard a voice that said, "If you don't speak to him, you will miss out on something good."

What? I glanced around to confirm that this wasn't some outside voice telling me what to do. No. This voice was a whisper that came from my heart. It was that inner wisdom, that personal North Star, that has proven its wisdom over and over again throughout my life.

The universe presented me a choice and I chose love.

My mind raced through every woman's magazine I'd ever read about how to start conversations with handsome young men, and I drew a blank. Then I went for the obvious. I ordered a cup of coffee too.

My cup arrived, I took a sip and then turned to him and said, "My. This stuff's strong, isn't it?" I may have even batted my 23-year-old eyelashes. He grabbed the hook, and I set it as we settled into a long conversation.

That conversation began a 40-year partnership filled with not only bone rattling ups and downs but also love, respect and a shared vision to make the world better in any way we were called to do.

We talked, we loved, and we married. Then he was gone. James died in 2018. He slipped away surrounded with people and music he loved. It was a good death following a long, difficult fight against rare thymic cancer.

Call it luck or call it blessed. We had a good marriage. I liken us to two oxen yoked together. Over the course of our life together sometimes he pulled the load and sometimes it was up to me. However, making a better life for our sons was our guiding star as we made our way through life's ups and downs. We did everything together and he knew me better than anybody except my mama.

And now he was gone, and I was left to carry the load alone.

That is a challenge that every widow or widower knows too well. Over 60% of my life was spent in a particular way and in a particular role. Suddenly it was gone, and I was faced with a decision.

Was I going to fully live the life I had left, or would I curl up on the sofa and wait for my late husband to come and fetch me?

I made my choice on a day I was feeling particularly low. My younger son called from many states away and he heard something different in my voice. I had done a good job of maintaining the façade but not so much that day. He was concerned, so in a stern voice, he said, "Mother, get off the couch. Get off the couch now."

That was it. My moment of choice came, and not only did I get off the couch I took the first step out of my malaise and turned toward a new way of life. It took a while but just as clearly as that voice once spoke to me, I knew that the way ahead was to feel the pain and survive despite it.

Otherwise, this grief would win.

Gratitude

WHAT DOES 'HOME' mean to you? Is it a place, a feeling, or something else entirely?

Most of my life, I've lived away from my place of origin, my home. Of course, 'home' can be defined by any number of factors and be in any number of places.

Over the years, I've been an official resident of seven different states, ranging from New York City to a small farm outside of Nashville, Tennessee. I've had houses I loved and cried over upon leaving, and others that were a relief to shed. Some I called home for a time.

Yet, when caring for my terminally ill husband, I once again came to where my people were. We needed help, and as Carl Sandberg says in his poem, *Death of a Hired Man*, "Home is the place where, when you have to go there, they have to take you in.'

Maybe that's so, but my experience of home is also reflected in the next few lines, 'I should have called it something you somehow haven't to deserve.'

Roots, Riverboats, and Dreamers

My home roots run deep in this river town. My people were riverboat people. The generations before me are buried in the middle of town, in a cemetery that once lay on its outskirts.

I was always a bit of a wanderer. I bounced around the country, trying out different versions of myself. But when homesickness caught up with me, I always thought of my riverboat town, flooded with memories of happy meals around the family table.

Each time I returned they welcomed me. Each time I was embraced. Each time I was restored.

How lucky I am to have known love from the crazy, fractured family that I call my own. I come from a family of teachers, artists, salesmen and at least one good cook. They each followed their dreams, and they always encouraged me to follow mine.

You want to go to New Orleans to a very expensive school to major in something completely irrational? Sure! Follow your heart!

You want to go to New York and try to become a professional actress? Sure! Follow your heart!

You want to answer a call to ministry? Sure! Follow your heart, but please accept people as they are and leave your judgements at the door.

That's what they did for me. They left their judgements at the door. They accepted my journey and the good and bad decisions along the way. They accepted me just as I am.

All the Body Holds

When I stood at their doorstep with a dying husband and overwhelmed by life, they said, "Sure! Welcome home."

It was at this home, I learned about unconditional love.

Clare Biedenharn, DMin, BCC

Not long ago, I attended a workshop led by Bessel van der Kolk, based on his book, *The Body Keeps the Score*. His scientifically researched theory states that when life slams us with trauma, our body holds the memory. This memory is a trigger that throws us back into trauma. Our bodies remember as they prepare to survive once again.

Perhaps the body holds something else as well. Just as it remembers the trauma, I wonder if the body holds the love that created us and sustained us. We forget about it. We take it for granted. We lose sight of what a treasure it is.

Yet that love remains like an underground spring that continues to flow, whether we're aware of it or not. It's there and it's up to us to remember it and give thanks for its bounty.

I give thanks. Not everyone grew up in a family like mine. Call it a blessing or luck. I know the unconditional love that shaped me was an incredible gift.

Of course, I didn't have a perfect childhood. I've had my own fair share of therapy, but as I look back, it is the love that I now remember.

Once, after my mother had slipped me a little cash to help pay a bill, I asked her how I could ever repay her for this and for so many other kindnesses. She smiled and told me the wisdom passed to her by her mother. "You help others as you have been helped."

Expression of true gratitude is simple.

"Pass it on."

Enjoy and replicate. Give thanks and remember how you were once helped and loved. Simple gestures hold great power.

"Pass it on."

And now, I'll give the key to you.

Pass it on.

Empty Monuments

"Looks like I've got everything I wanted to get."

My friend closed the car trunk filled with a few remnants of her parents' lives. She sighed as she said her good-byes. She'd inherited this place and over the years it had been good. Now it was a little too far from her home and a little too much to maintain. Her brother encouraged her to sell it. He said, "I have my memories. That's all I need."

I went with her to the bank when she signed the contract. Just like her, the house was beginning a new era. She said she was at peace as she released her last physical connection to her love-filled family past. On the drive back home, we listened to old songs and reminisced about endings and beginnings.

I shared how my last move had been one of my biggest life challenges. My husband was dying. We needed help. So, we walked away from the life we loved in New Orleans and moved back to my childhood home where we were surrounded by supportive family.

Decades of my mother, my mother-in-law and my aunt's treasures were now my burden. Each piece, each box, required a decision. For me, the question was not just one of how I was going to move from one house to another half its size. The true question about everything I touched was, "Will it stay, or will it go?"

It was awful.

I had to decide. What did all this seemingly important clutter really mean? What did this stuff represent to me?

I'd loved these women. They were important to me. Their presence was palpable in every vase, pan or flowerpot. To toss their 'treasures' was like losing them all over again. Yet hard decisions had to be made.

I began with Christmas decorations. That was a good place to start because it forced me into a reality check. Our life was facing massive change. I culled through the boxes and brought only those ornaments that were important to me.

From that shaky beginning, I was able to let go of my mother's patio furniture and bunk beds that my now adult sons had slept in decades ago. My grandmother's dining room table was too big for our new home. When I realized that I was the only one who remembered the ghosts of loved ones who sat around it long ago, it was a little easier to release it.

I must admit it. I felt relief as my physical footprint grew lighter.

There are a few regrets. I chose my 'good' China that I never really liked over my favorite everyday plates. There was only room for one bike and even though my husband could no longer ride I knew how important his bike was to him. My beloved college bike stayed.

As I faced an overwhelming task, I had to ask myself some tough questions. Did these important ladies want their 'treasures' to bring me such heartache? No. Do I want my children to have to wrestle with my treasures? No.

I've seen old photographs of pianos abandoned as wagon trains inched their way to a new life in the West. The horse drawn wagons began the journey filled with what was once considered to be the bare necessities, but as the wagon train went on for months, and travel became more difficult, non-essentials were tossed. Personal priorities changed.

Priorities changed for me too as I realized that it wasn't the material things I held in my heart. The true value lies in the memories they evoked.

I agree with my friend's brother. I have my memories and that is enough. It pleases me to know that other boys sleep in the bunk beds that were standing empty and another family breaks bread around my grandmother's table. The value for me lies in those memories created for others.

And I am free.

PART II

Grief is More Than a Thing
GRIEVING

Stone of Grief

My phone rang suddenly, and I jumped. I glanced at the number and didn't recognize it. My thought was that this was probably just another call from a telemarketer selling unwanted car warranties. I hesitated but then I thought, "The call *might* be important."

Before long I felt like I was on the TV show *Dragnet* as I tried to discern "just the facts, ma'am. Just the facts." Little did I know what I was beginning. This was to be a challenge that needed to be addressed.

I answered and identified myself. An unfamiliar voice answered, "We are an assisted care facility. I know from your book that you work primarily with nurses. Would you consider working with our leadership team? We are stuck in grief, and we need to recalibrate after the pandemic."

Stuck in grief? That sounded uncomfortably familiar. Recalibration? That's something I can understand.

Grief is a sticky emotion. It doesn't disappear like fairy footprints in the garden. When it chooses to come, it aims right for your heart to wrestle you down to the ground. Unlike feelings evoked from memories of things that brought you happiness, grief is raw, and the feelings are just as real as when your loss first happened.

I know a little about grief. First as a critical care chaplain and then working with organ donor families, I have decades of experience. I've held hands and dried tears for many as they faced one of life's biggest mysteries: death.

Then things got personal. My husband was diagnosed with rare thymic cancer that, over time, resulted in his death.

I write that statement from my head.

My heart wants to tell you about the remarkable person he was.

My heart wants to share how speaking to a good-looking guy over a cup of coffee in New Orleans led to over 40 years of shared experience of love and respect.

My heart prefers to forget the vascular dementia brought on by heart failure from every treatment we could think of.

My heart prefers to forget the last days of 'terminal restlessness' as his body thrashed around in the bed preparing to let go of life.

My heart…oh, my heart.

Oh, sure. I've studied Elisabeth Kubler-Ross's work with the dying that spelled out stages of grief. I give thanks for her groundbreaking work that opened the door to talking about death and dying. Her studies focused on grief of those approaching death but over time stages of grief filtered into broader use.

If only it were so easy.

- denial
- anger
- bargaining
- depression
- acceptance

I've felt all of those, but those feelings are only phase one.

Clare Biedenharn, DMin, BCC

The Ripples of Grief

There's also anticipatory grief that comes with the realization that the life story with the happily-ever-after ending isn't going to be the one you get.

There is grief from watching a vibrant, healthy loved one dissolve before your eyes as you stand by absolutely helpless.

There is the grief that comes from seeing someone you care for suffer physically, emotionally and spiritually. Fortunately, my husband was solid in his faith, so I was spared watching that disintegrate too.

There is the grief of leaving a job and a city I loved, moving from our newly renovated "forever" home to be near the family support we needed to make it through that last, hard stretch.

There is grief in deaths coming so fast – mother, brother, husband and even my dog—that there was hardly time to grieve one before the next one was gone

Stuck in grief? I've got this.

- Primary grief is the loss of someone or something dear to you.
- Secondary grief refers to the ongoing process of grieving everything else.

Primary grief is the stone tossed into a quiet pond.

Secondary grief is the resulting ripples emanating from that stone breaking the surface of the water.

Loss of something important lies at the root of grief. For some it's the loss of a job or a lifestyle. It's all personal, but my losses centered on people.

I had a full understanding of the initial blast of grief that comes with the loss of a loved one. What I wasn't expecting was that next tier of grief. I thought grief was the loss of someone you love and that was it. But the loss shows up in other ways too.

Place in society

The advice to wait a year after your loss before you do anything is valid. Nothing makes sense that first year.

Remember anger in the Kubler-Ross list of grief responses? Mine showed up in full force soon after James' death.

Here I was looking at a form I had to fill out for some essential reason or another. The questions asked my relationship status. My encounter with the form did not begin well. Before I knew it, I was screaming at this piece of paper that was obviously composed by someone with little life experience particularly in the area of death.

The question "What is your relationship status?' is very common but the responses were limited to:

- Married
- Divorced
- Single

What happened to the category: Widowed?

I yelled at the piece of paper called a form. I had been unexpectedly thrown deep into the quagmire question of where my place is now in the world. When did the word 'widow' fall off the map?

I am single but not by choice. I had been half of a marriage for over 40 years. Now, suddenly I had to find my way to establish who I was separate from my mate, my pal, my partner. I felt abandoned and discounted by a world that avoids the subject of death.

I'm a widow and I demand respect.

Financial Security

I was more fortunate than many. My husband was on Social Security so I could claim his benefits. But what about households that depend on a single salary or government benefit? In my work as chaplain, I often saw this fear bubble up for families following a bike or motorcycle accident. Where's the next paycheck coming from? How are we going to pay for the funeral? Results of that single death reverberated through the generations. Spouse, children, as well as extended families are faced with an unexpected loss of income. How will we survive?

Fear of the Future

Who, what, why, when, where? These are life's ongoing questions but without the comfort of someone to make decisions with you, choices may feel overwhelming.

When my husband died, I was at a crossroad. One road ended in being stuck in grief. He was gone and not coming back.

What was I to do? What would I choose? Was I going to live or was I going to die? It wouldn't be physical death, but I could easily have shut down, sat on the couch eating junk food and watching TV waiting for James to come get me.

Or would I take the other road? Would I choose life?

Reflect, Reconnect & Restore

In a way that phone call opened my eyes to the grief that is endemic in the post lockdown COVID world.

My grief was personal but if we care about the work we do, isn't that personal too? If we are challenged to step into new roles while we leave our old ones, isn't that personal grief? Or maybe we just miss how life used to be and wished it could all go back the way it was. That longing is grief as well.

As I spoke to the head of the assisted care facility, I could see that the leadership team had suffered losses similar to mine. The healthcare world as they knew it had been stripped away by a disease that fought not just with a virus but with fear, unknowing, and loss of structure. Yet they handled their challenges beautifully and were able to maintain good quality care of their patients. Now it was time to shake off the past and find a new direction.

Grief is sticky but that doesn't mean that it can't be handled. I looked at my own stages of recovery and I saw what steps helped me most.

Reflect

I let the memories flood over me, and I willed myself to feel the pain. The pandemic lockdown shut off some of my favorite avenues to numbness like food or shoe shopping as I hunkered down in my little house. But I felt in my bones that the only way through to healing was to feel the pain and let it go. Otherwise, it would fester and show in other ways.

It wasn't easy. I especially dreaded what I called the "Blindside Hits." Tiny triggers that elicited waves of grief. Sometimes it was a song, or just a memory that popped up that brought me to my knees once again.

One day I was driving to a hospital for work when one of those hits t-boned me. I had to be focused for the work I did. I couldn't let this distract me. I pulled over and said out loud," Please stop the blindside hits. I can't take them anymore." They still show up but not as often and not as intensely. They show up as a nudge not a full body slam. That does make them easier to handle.

James really declined and before we knew it, he was at his end. For a while, all I could remember were the really hard times. I thought, "After 40 years, THIS is all I remember?" God's grace helped me through that one too. Gentle sharing of memories with longtime friends helped me anchor myself in the whole of our marriage, not just that last sliver of the time we had together.

Reconnect

A couple of years after James' death, I finally woke up. I thought of Sleeping Beauty waking up after her long, long slumber. In my mind I saw her stretch, rub her eyes, and look around to see a different world. I could hear her say, "What happened to those 100 years?"

My snooze was only a decade or so, but slowly I felt myself stepping back into life.

I realized my friends and family had carried me through this time of slumber and now they were tugging me back into the stream of life.

For me, the awakening was not dramatic. It was more like the seedling pushing up against the soil to grow toward the sun. Slowly, I regained my footing.

I joined my son and his family for Christmas a couple of years after James' death. We were chatting about different things, and I noticed them passing glances as we talked. I realized that something about me was different, and they weren't sure what to make of me. I said, "I see you exchanging glances. I guess I am different. I've decided that it's ok to be happy."

That was a turning point for me.

STONE OF GRIEF

Restore

I look back on the footprints I left in the dew of the morning grass. They still point forward. If I were to go back to them, I'd be facing in the wrong direction. I would also be blocking my growth along with the opportunities that come with it.

"It takes a while to back down from a fight." That's what my son said shortly after his father's death. We were sitting in the living room, and he noticed that I still cocked my ear toward the bedroom even though the funeral home had carried James' body away.

Listening for sounds from the next room was a habit that would take a while to break. Eventually I did. Change came slowly.

- I allowed myself to take as many naps as I could squeeze in once I realized I was exhausted from being on high alert for years.
- I replaced the hospital bed with a different one that James had never slept in.
- After a year, I removed my wedding ring.

Slow and steady wins the race.

And there was one more thing I did. The day I was defending my listening study in Chicago, James was getting his first of many scans in New Orleans. The news was not good, and I sealed up all my work and set it aside to give him my full attention.

James knew this work was important to me and he encouraged me to get back to my work on deep listening and I did.

It took me a while, but I wrote an Amazon best-selling book, *Heart to Heart: Spiritual Care through Deep Listening*. I am grateful for that project. That was my grief work and kept me on track as I grew stronger and recovered to recalibrate myself.

Clare Biedenharn, DMin, BCC

Perhaps grief is curled up inside of you waiting for just the right trigger to take you to your knees.

When it comes, feel it, and let the grief flow. The shortest way out is straight ahead.

And as one who has walked this road may I give you hope that, in time, things will get better.

After all, even those ripples in the pond find their way to the shore.

Salty Venice

CROSSING INTO THE COOL, humid air relieved me of the glaring outside heat and tourist noise. Now inside, I glanced around the historic San Marco Cathedral in Venice, Italy, and was surprised at the contrast between my 20-year-old memory and the space I was in now. Back then, the interior was much darker.

Now, wooden planks were scattered around the church to keep our feet dry. Water seeped up from between the cracks of the stone floor. It was then that I realized that much like New Orleans, Venice is a city floating on water.

Sections of the cathedral sit at or below sea level. The massive flood of 1966 broached the marble slabs perched on wood pilings. These protected the more porous brick from the marshy water on which the city is built. That breech accelerated the city's physical decline. The city's ancient pilings continue to sink into the marshy water on which the city is built.

The cathedral fights a simple but persistent enemy. The watery marshes that once protected Venice from invading hordes now carries another foe: salt.

SALTY VENICE

Salt

Humans can't survive without it. The balance between salt and potassium manages the fluids in our body. Too much salt is as bad as too little. Managing the middle is where health lies.

Salt was an essential element to the ancient world, which depended on salt for a range of tasks, from curing leather to preserving food in a world without refrigeration. Salt was such a valuable commodity that at one point it was used like money. Wars were fought over salt. Kingdoms were lost and won over salt.

Now it is salt that eats away at San Marco as the city sinks into the marshes. Saltwater wicks its way up, eats away at the mortar, and weakens the brick.

As the water evaporates, it leaves evidence of its presence. On exterior walls it shows as white, shadowy residue. In interior areas of the cathedral like the basement crypt, the residue reveals its presence through the appearance of a white, brittle lace on the walls and columns.

Those white lacy Venetian columns came to mind not long ago, while lying in bed. Tears made their way from my eyes to my pillow: once again, life without my life partner seemed just a bit overwhelming. Once again, some trigger surfaced to surprise me. Much like the water wicking up the columns from the marshy depths, my tears bubbled up from some deep place to be released to my pillow.

My pillow, my friend, has captured and held many of my tears, and it was at that moment I considered how many tears it could hold before it became crusty with salt like those columns found in the crypt of San Marco.

Then I wondered: if I didn't release my tears, would I hold that salt of sorrow instead and become as brittle as those columns? The image of closely held tears working their way through from my core to my skin came to me, and suddenly an Old Testament story startled me. If I didn't let the tears flow, if I continued to hold them in, would I one day become a pillar of salt like Lot's wife looking back as she was leaving her past?

On Grief

It's been five years since my husband's death. Some might say I've grieved long enough. Some might tell me to just move on. It is hard to just walk away from a relationship whose span covered 60% of my life. This relationship we shared was close and together, we rode out the highs and the lows that appear in any life.

Those undulations of life continue but now I'm navigating alone. It was scary at first, but as Louisa May Alcott wrote, "I am not afraid of storms because I am learning how to sail my ship."

At some point, I transitioned from deeply grieving to merely grieving. There finally came a day when I realized I had not mentioned his name or told a story about him for at least a day, maybe two.

He was sick for a long time. He suffered. That's not the part that I miss. In fact, I am grateful that he died before the pandemic lockdown.

What I grieve for is the time before the illness. I grieve more for "my" funny, loving husband who occasionally surfaced from the heart failure fog at the end of his life. And to be honest I grieve for that moment in time when we and our high school sons were home, and we were together as a family. I grieve for a moment in time, a memory.

Grief sets its own rules. The tears come less often, but they still surface unexpectedly. The trigger comes and then the tears. It may be a memory that activates the grief, but when it comes it's not as some fuzzy moment from the past. No. It comes as fresh and hot and real as the first moment when it came to call. No wonder people want to avoid it.

Some tell those who grieve that it's time to move on. But grief for me, has found its place and I accommodate it. I can live with it. I acknowledge it, but it doesn't rule my life as it did for quite a while.

Crying may not be pretty, but I embrace grief and its tears because I know that the path ahead includes snotty noses and tear-stained faces. The path ahead leads through damp, salty pillows and the catharsis that comes from a good, deep cry.

What happens when we don't release our tears? What does sorrow waiting for release do to our body?

If I don't release my salty tears, if I hold them in because I am afraid of such strong emotion, will I become as brittle as those columns holding up San Marco Cathedral? Or can my tears cleanse my soul and help me find my peace?

I appreciate the tears and thank them for not coming quite so frequently, but they are welcome when they do come. In them lies my release and my healing.

Thank you, my salty friends.

Stone and Kin

TOMORROW MY SISTER and I have an unusual appointment. Together we're going to order a headstone for our paternal grandparents, Robert and Clara, who died back in the 1940s.

They died before either of us was born and for whatever reason, unlike my mother's family, we didn't know much about Daddy's folks. I'd heard that Grandmother Clara died of cancer while my mother was pregnant with my sister. And then there was the story of my grandfather passing away in a room he rented from my other grandparents, Nonnie and Poppie, that made it into the family stories. Other than two half-sisters who lived away, there wasn't much information about Clara, the grandmother for whom I was named.

This journey began years ago when I Googled my father's name. My grandfather's name popped up too. I was surprised because that side of the family was always a bit of a mystery and, to be perfectly honest, I kind of forgot about him and Clara.

A picture smiled back at me from the computer screen, and I saw the strong resemblance that laced its way from grandfather to my father and then to me. My sister is petite and lady-like and favored my mother's side of the family. I, on the other hand, was the only one of his children who looked like Daddy. I was the tallest one in my class and had my daddy's eyebrows.

Who did my grandmother look like? I've never seen her picture.

Daddy spoke well of his parents but other than a name, I'm not sure if he shared much with the people he came from. He didn't tell their stories. So, over time, they were lost. And when the stories and the memories they evoke disappear, it is like the person is lost as well.

I was visiting my parent's grave one day when I suddenly thought about my 'other' grandparents. I knew through the internet that my grandfather was in the same cemetery. But my grandmother? I wasn't sure.

The man at the cemetery office looked them up in his well-worn book. My grandparents were buried side by side and he offered to show me their graves. It was at that moment that I was flabbergasted to learn that they were only a few yards from my parents' and grandparents' plots. I had driven by them a hundred times, but I wouldn't have known because they didn't have a headstone. They were buried in an unmarked grave. That was about to change.

"I wonder how they met," Cousin Molly asked when I reached out to find out Clara's exact birthday for the headstone we would be ordering. She was a distant cousin I only recently found that I had. I connected through the one cousin I did know about. Cousin Lynne and I knew each other growing up but lost contact after high school.

I heard Lynne was in the hospital and decided that this was a time to reconnect. I hesitantly knocked on the door not knowing what to expect but she greeted me with a smile and a big "hello." I was surprised. Even after a long illness her height, big bones and tall forehead mirrored my own. I resonated with this woman in the bed. I felt I had finally found 'my' people, my tribe. I'd found my place.

Cousin Molly, who looks much like Lynne and me, loves genealogy so it was to her I turned to find Clara's birthdate. We had the month and year but not the day. It was Molly who asked the question about how my grandparents met. I not only didn't know the answer, but I realized that there were so many things unknown to me about my father's side of the family. I didn't learn the stories and now they are gone.

In the Old Testament days of the Bible, a stone was placed and a new name given at the site of a significant event. Maybe that is the source of putting a piece of rock on someone's grave. It says, "This person was significant. This person was real."

Headstones perhaps don't carry the importance they once did. The practice of cremation and scattering ashes is well accepted. To my grandparents' generation, however, a good death included a nice burial and a headstone. Perhaps they couldn't get one then, but they will in the spring when the winter ground thaws, and the stone is installed.

I am not sure why this is important to me. I am not sure why placing a headstone wasn't important to my father. For me, maybe it's a sense of responsibility for the unknown tribe that I now realize that I am a part of. It feels good to honor my ancestors and I am grateful that my sister and I can see this task to completion.

People came before you and me and there are those who will come after us. We are one link in a chain whose beginning was farther back than we will ever know. The chain continues after us as well.

Do you know the stories of your ancestors? It sounds so formal, but those tales are hidden in memories of past Christmases or family holidays. Those tales are a glue of shared experience that helped create the person you became. There is strength in that glue, and it is important to see that your children discover it too.

And for the ones who follow, it is important to not only share those stories but create new ones as well. Be intentional because it is through those memories that you will live on.

Bandwidth and Scarcity

MY 20-YEAR-OLD TOYOTA HIGHLANDER has remarkable amenities that include an FM/AM radio, CD player AND a cassette player.

One evening as I was rummaging through my purse my 4-year-old grandson spotted a cassette tape that I'd stuck in my purse to listen to on my hours long drive to his house. He was captivated with this odd black rectangle of plastic that had some kind of brown tape that moved if you turned either of the white wheels. He had never seen such a thing. So, of course he immediately wanted to see how it worked. It was already dark outside so I promised that we would check it out in the morning.

The next morning just as I was pouring my first cup of coffee he popped up from out of nowhere. "Grandma, can we try that plastic thing now? PLEASE?"

I grabbed my keys and as I helped him climb up into the car he said, "I just don't get how it works, Grandma."

I turned the ignition key, inserted the tape into the player, and suddenly the music blasted out.

He stared at the console intently for about 30 seconds and then the moment was over. Too bad it was classical music. I might have captured his attention for a full minute if I'd played a children's song. For just that brief moment I watched his focused attention as his brain tried to solve the equation.

Weird plastic thing + car that has a hole to gobble it up = noise.

The moment was gone. His curiosity was satisfied, and he moved on and he never mentioned it again.

If the event captured his attention and drew him into engagement, we could say he put it in his bandwidth. Instead, he processed the information and then deleted what he didn't need. He had no attachment to what he saw so he let it go without any further interest in the cassette or the player.

Bandwidth

The word bandwidth comes from electronics and has worked its way into everyday language. It is a term that describes how much information can be transmitted electronically within a given amount of time.

Has this ever happened to you? At the same time, you are watching a movie your son is playing an online game, and your daughter is researching some homework online. Suddenly the screen image seems to stumble, and a message informs you that there is a problem. Too much information Is trying to come in at the same time. There is not enough bandwidth.

The internet doesn't prioritize the importance of each task. Everything, whether it is a movie, online game or download is the same to it and it will handle as much as you demand of it until it cannot carry anything else. That's when somebody needs to stop doing something!

Another kind of bandwidth

We can use the word bandwidth in a different way too. Dictionary.com describes it as "the energy or mental capacity required to deal with a situation." That means each task carries a certain amount of energy and, like filling a bucket to the brim, sometimes we just top out as we reach our physical emotional or spiritual limit.

The phrase "I'm on overload" means your bandwidth is at full capacity. You have nothing else to give even though the demands keep coming.

Complicated life

We live complicated lives with increasing demands. It's not only our jobs that put demands on us, but as you pay for childcare, stretch the paycheck to cover the bills, grocery shop while staying strong and awake enough to engage with the family over a meal, your bandwidth can fill very quickly.

Different point of view

When our bandwidth is full it affects how we see our world.

In a study of how poverty might affect decision-making, two Princeton University professors, Shafir and Mullainathian questioned in their book, *Scarcity*, basic assumptions about the basis of poverty. They question if our understanding of the concept was too limited to that of poor values and lack of planning.

They created a study on stress and decision-making using a game scenario similar to the game show "Family Feud." One team was set up as 'poor' and the other as 'rich.' With the clock ticking each faced limited solutions that included taking out a high interest paycheck loan.

Their studies showed that when we feel like we don't have enough then we focus on the lack. The more we focus on the lack then our focus clogs up our bandwidth and it affects our decisions. Just like the junk that clogs pipes, the focus on paying the bills, not getting the lights cut off, and buying books for the kids for school can clog up our ability to make good decisions.

Have you ever faced something like this?

You may not believe this has much to do with you but what if we applied this in a different way. Rather than the question being that of money, what if we applied this psychology of scarcity to you and your capacity to handle your job, your patients, your family, or your life?

In what way is your stress level affecting your ability to make clear decisions? When you feel stressed to the max, when you look around and only see not enough time or resources, you may not be so different from the person facing the question of paying their bills.

You may be on overload and on the edge of making some bad decisions. Scarcity is a mindset that can affect every part of your life not only by your decisions but by the energy you carry with you.

For the nurse: I have so much to do and so little time! I worry about patient safety!

For the administrator: They ask too much of me! I can't squeeze blood out of a turnip!

For the essential worker: At what point can I just say, "No. I've done enough."

For the parent: What do you mean you need money for new soccer cleats to match the team! The electric bill is due!

For the child: What else do you want me to cram into a day?

So how can you be sure that there's enough of you for you. You feel dried up. How do you fill your well?

Maybe the place to start is to approach the question like a 4-year-old.

- He prioritized all the stimuli confronting him.
- He determined that the results did not have a direct connection to what he needed or wanted.
- He let it go and he didn't look back.

Those steps might work for you. Some things you can let go. That's a place to start.

And wish me luck. Next time I'm going to introduce my grandson to the car's CD player. Maybe that will capture his imagination.

PART III

When I Became a Butterfly
TRANSFORMATION

Cocoon

I HAD a little dose of reality last week as my granddaughter and I watched the last of the four butterflies emerge from their chrysalis or cocoon. They came in an Easter kit that contains everything needed to support the butterfly as it transitions from one way of life to another. The chrysalis looks like mud daubers' nests clinging to a piece of cardboard in a soft cage filled with sticks and grass. When the butterflies emerge small pieces of fruit nourish them until they can be released.

The idea of coming out of a cocoon to emerge as a butterfly is a bit romantic. There is the little cocoon and then the fluttering wings. What I forgot was just how messy coming out of the cocoon can be.

"Ooo!! There's a spot of blood!!" my five-year-old granddaughter squealed. She gave me one of her most skeptical looks as I assured her that butterflies do not have blood. I don't blame her. The slime dripping from the empty cocoon was pretty gross and the butterfly's wings barely moved until they dried out a bit.

There is a certain amount of grunt work in transition. Going from point A to point B sounds simple but the actual work involved can be challenging. Ask a six-year-old.

Another granddaughter read to me a story from a book that has more pictures than words. The story was how the elephant saved all the fish from a shark. Slowly she sounded out words like, "the," "fish," and "hid." Then at the end of the story, she showed me her book journal that she turns in to her teacher every week. Each page has lines where she writes a statement about the book and then space where she can draw a picture.

Later I looked at her journal more closely. As I held it and flipped through the pages, I was reminded of a flip animation book, where each page holds a picture that is just a little different from the one before. As you flip through the book the eye fills the gaps and the figure appears to move forward just like a cartoon.

My granddaughter began her journal earlier in the year and I saw how slowly but surely each page reflected just a bit more confidence than the one before. Page one was barely legible. In fact, as she showed it to me, even she had trouble making out the words. Gradually over time her pictures and her writing transitioned from the barely legible to the somewhat clear. Most importantly, she could now read her own words and explain what she wrote. That was progress. That was transformation.

The journal pages kicked up a little bit of wind as I flipped quickly through the book, and I thought of the slight breeze the butterfly needed to dry out its wings. In a way, each was preparation for its own kind of flight.

The journal will be tucked away waiting to be rediscovered one day. The very literate young lady will smile and remember how limited her now polished skills once were. What was once hard is now easy. What was once scary, whether learning to read or emerging from a cocoon, is now an accomplished task.

It is easy to focus on one's own limitations in the face of a task and in the struggle forget the truth.

Clare Biedenharn, DMin, BCC

Change happens. Transformation comes. Sometimes it is messy like the slimy cocoon as the butterfly stretches and dries its wings. Sometimes it comes slowly, like one book, one story, one page at a time. Like the cartoon figure in the flip book, we need change to move forward as we adapt and thrive.

Fall Colors
FAMILIAR SEASONS

1... 2... 3... 4... 5... How can there be so many fall shades of yellow?

I took in the exquisite fall colors surrounding me, as I sat at an interstate rest stop on the border of Minnesota.

Only yesterday, I was home, further south where the trees were just beginning to consider their fall attire. Today, I counted the big splashes of color embracing the air around me.

Less than six months ago, I celebrated spring, singing its promise through its full range of delicate greens, pinks and yellows. Suddenly, summer's hot colors and glaring sunlight arrived with their intense yellows, reds, and deep green. Almost overnight, it's fall. The trees become brightly colored. In preparation for the next step in the circle of seasons, their life force returns to its roots.

Then comes winter. The trees become barren. In my part of the world, the days are shrouded in gray for weeks at a time.

Each season brings its gifts. The greatest is the gift of rhythm and predictability. There is comfort in predictability. No matter what events spin around us, day still follows night. Spring leads to summer, which in turn becomes fall.

And then, there's winter. The time of the year when the earth and her inhabitants hunker down and know in full faith that eventually spring will emerge, and the cycle begins again.

A part of me dreads the coming winter, with its memories of ice storms, snow, and power outages. Cold, gray days often seem interminable, just like their litany of scraping icy windshields and sprinkling salt on the sidewalks.

Still, winter brings its gifts. Even in winter there is growth. Underground, the tree roots prepare themselves to push life once again into the tree branches.

Life is there, but hidden, preparing to re-emerge. If it's true for trees, it can be true for people too.

Seasons of Life

Ten years ago, my life changed. My husband was diagnosed with terminal cancer. Cancer is what happens when the rhythm of life is altered. What should be dependable is not.

He fought hard and I was his number one cheerleader, but it came to the point where we needed help. We moved closer to family. In that process, we left my dream job in my dream town and a home whose renovation was completed just before the diagnosis. As James slipped away at home surrounded by people who loved him, I knew that this move was essential for us both.

But that wasn't all. Within a space of two years, my husband, my mother, my brother, and my dog died.

That's when my winter began.

Just like the sap withdraws to protect its strength, I withdrew. My little bungalow home became my hermitage, my safe place, to recover from a wounded heart.

I'm not the same person I was when my husband and I moved into this little cottage seven years ago. It's been five years since his death. Now something is finally beginning to stir in me.

Each Season Has Its Gifts

Winter will soon be here, and while it may seem bleak and long, I find solace in acknowledging this dormant time of quiet growth.

Like Sleeping Beauty after her decades-long nap, I've had my waking moment. With it comes an affectionate embrace of the past followed by release.

I miss those whom I've lost. I miss the job I loved and my wonderful former home. That home was for a different season of life, however. My little gray bungalow is what I needed for my season of winter and recovery.

My surroundings may soon be wrapped in winter, but I know in my heart that spring is already stirring within me. I look forward, with anticipation and hope, to whatever the next season may bring.

Steps of Change

CHRISTMAS 2019 IS NOW a rosy memory. Little did we know how close we were to profound, unsettling change as the COVID 19 pandemic creeped into 2020 and quickly stole away our normal. Now, no matter what we may hope for, we know that life won't ever quite be the same.

The Oxford Dictionary describes a paradigm shift as "a fundamental change in approach or underlying assumptions." In other words, our world, our rules and our expectations have changed on every possible level.

Life is now like that moment when we first step from the solid dock into a small boat. One moment we were on solid ground. The next we're trying to find the balance that will keep us from falling over the side and into the water. This boat we all share feels unsteady as we try to find our balance in this new life. We're in the process and we will find it. It's that adaptation to change that has sustained our human race.

We all face change. In my book "Heart to Heart: Spiritual Care through

Deep Listening,"* I tell of the day my husband decided to enter treatment for alcoholism. We sat in the marriage counselor's office to figure out our messy life when out of the blue James said, "I think I may have developed a drinking problem."

That one statement changed the life trajectory for him and for our family. Nothing would ever be the same. As scary as it was, ultimately it was a very good thing.

Francis Coombs and Theresa Nemeck describe in their classic book, "The Spiritual Journey," three critical moments that we cross as we grow. The moments are like the threshold of a doorway as we move from one stage of life to the next.

They describe three thresholds considered critical to human development.

1. *They are radical.* James didn't weigh the repercussions. He didn't stop to wonder how I would react. He was fighting for his life, and we were welcomed to come along with him. To admit a problem like that creates change right down to the molecular level.
2. *They are irreversible.* Once he named the problem, there was no going back. "The cat was out of the bag," and no way it could go back in. His admission was a stone tossed in a pond. The ripples move out from the central point. Were we, as a family, willing to change too?
3. *They are successive.* One threshold builds on the previous one and opens the path to another. It's like climbing a ladder one rung at a time. Consistency is hard, but it is essential for lasting change. That's one of the biggest challenges for all of us.

For me denial came first. Then came fear as I realized that this change in direction required me to face my place in our story. That change also

---

* Heart to Heart: Spiritual Care through Deep Listening, Clare Biedenharn brought hope for a way out of our mired down life. Our hope for a better life for our children did something else. Hope motivated us, kept us going, and birthed us into something new. We did the work, and we got better.

Here is the big question for you. Do you see some area of your life that needs a change? More importantly are you willing to make that change? Are you willing to try something new?

Small change counts. Even taking a different way home creates a new perspective.

Or maybe your life is like a too small coat, and you are ready for a big change.

We live in dynamic times and the one thing that never changes is our ability to choose. Change includes choice. Are you ready?

The answer lies within you.

Silent Growth

ONCE AGAIN I was in Dallas for summer school and our class was following a hand drawn map to visit a community center. A small wavy line marked the Trinity River, but in my three summers I had yet to see a drop of rain. I was curious what a river in this hot, dry town might be.

Our line of cars crossed on a narrow bridge that was, according to the sign, the Trinity River. All I saw below was some dried grass and maybe a tree. The long bridge stretched ahead and before I knew it, we were sitting at a stoplight on the OTHER side of the bridge. Did I miss something? If there was a river there, I sure didn't see it.

My idea of a river was more like the mighty Mississippi that passed near my home in Vicksburg, at the southern end of the verdant Mississippi Delta. Every day 48% of the freshwater on the North American continent sweeps by on its way to the Gulf of Mexico.

Unlike the exposed dry bed called Trinity, the Mississippi may appear placid but underneath the river teems with life. Giant catfish swim through it. Tugboats carry coal. And boaters know it as a deceptive place where seemingly innocent eddies can suck full-sized trees underwater to suddenly pop to the surface miles downstream. How could two rivers be so different?

As I rode back over that dry ditch of a river the idea came to me that maybe they weren't so different. Perhaps once upon a time the Mississippi River looked just like this. One small creek fed into a larger one until slowly, over millions of years, that small stream became the river it is today.

The change didn't come fast. It only came with time.

Time is one of those things we never seem to have enough of as we rush to work, rush to take the kids to practice or as we sit with a tapping foot in line at the nearby fast-food restaurant.

The pandemic forced a different type of time on us as it took away our distractions. Instead of handing the kids their dinner in a paper bag, we sat together at a table and shared a meal face to face. Ordinary trips to the assisted care facility became a treasured time for each person to fully look into the face of a loved one if only through a pane of glass. Everyday moments reminded us of their sacredness as we drew in for the quiet time. Everything was suddenly different. Life changed. At first it felt catastrophic but over time our lives adapted to the change.

Our personal version of catastrophe came years earlier in the form of James' terminal cancer diagnosis. Just as some are fighting today to regain their pre-pandemic lives, we fought hard to hang on to our life together even as it slipped away. We maintained our placid surface as best we could but underneath, we adapted to our uncomfortable emerging life one stream, one creek, one raindrop at a time. Each doctor's visit eroded our hope. We prepared for change as best we could.

James was a patient man, so it surprised me when he uncharacteristically fussed at me about my attitude. He was right. I was different.

I told him, "This disease of yours has changed you and it has changed me. I've become the person I need to be to fight for you."

My declaration surprised me as well as him. Change had been subtle in us both. We grew less like flashy flowers and more like tree roots growing under the ground while snow and ice danced over them.

I felt strong as I realized that even in the face of sorrow, frustration, grief and terror somehow, I had grown. Something was different within me and whatever that was I was better prepared to face the inevitable end when he died four years later. I coped and reluctantly, I survived.

As we gingerly slip back into some semblance of normal life, turn your eyes from the past and look to who you are now and what you want for your future. Consider your gains as well as your losses and use this opportunity to consider how you want your 'normal' to be.

- In what quiet ways have you grown?
- What are you willing to let go?
- What is important to you now?
- What are you willing to fight to keep?

We live in a dynamic age. The Mississippi River took its time to become what it is today, but that growth hasn't been a luxury we could enjoy. The world has changed. You have changed. Growth continues. It may very well be like winter growth. We don't see it because it's not yet ready to reveal itself but it's there.

PART IV

Coming Back to Center
MENTAL WELL-BEING

What Is Your Worst Nightmare

WHAT IS YOUR WORST NIGHTMARE? You know, the kind that startles you awake with your heart racing.

For me, it's the one where I'm standing on stage. I am alone. The curtain rises and the crowd hangs on my opening words. Onstage. Alone.

The worst possible thing happens. I can't remember any of my lines of the play.

Or have you ever had this bone-rattling dream? You are sitting ready to take a test. You stare at the blank paper and suddenly you realize that you not only don't know any of the answers, but you also have no idea, earthly idea about where to begin. Your mind draws a blank. You are sunk.

Feelings Of Fear and Panic

The feelings are fear, panic, and even more, the baseline is the realization that you are not perfect. You are not enough. You've been found out for who you really know you are.

Feelings like that don't just happen in dreams. They come to the ballplayer who misses the game-winning toss or the person who finds their checking account overdrawn.

And for the nurse and nursing staff, those feelings can come at beside as the patient or loved one looks at you and says, "What would you do if this were your family?"

Many would offer an opinion. Many would want to jump in and 'fix' the problem as you nimbly think fast on your feet and come up with your best possible solution.

But what we do and what we think we would do can be two very different things. On a recent NPR.org podcast, *Hidden Brain*, Shankar Vedantam presented studies that discussed what is called the 'Hot/Cold Empathy Gap.' The studies show that our logical self can effectively line out a plan of action that is completely lost once you are in the middle of strong emotions such as anger, fear or sexual arousal. Our strong emotions disconnect us from our logical side of our brain.

Vedantam uses the example of the comedienne Morgan Smalley who left her venue following a stellar performance. She hit the proverbial ball out of the park that night and as she left, she was basking in the glow of the perfect evening.

A man approached her with some random junky items in a shoebox. There were some pens, an Amazon gift card, a pair of shoes that weren't even her size. The man said he'd sell the box to her for $25. She laughed and said sure. After all, she was on a roll!

Even though it was late, and she didn't know this man she took him to her ATM where she could only get withdrawal in increments of $20. She asked if he would sell her the stuff for $20 and he said no. So, she withdrew $40 and gave it to him for a shoebox of items most likely swiped from unlocked cars.

But as she told her family when she got home, "But he was such a nice guy!" In her aroused state following her great performance she completely lost track of her logical self.

It happened to her. It can happen to you.

How to Handle Nightmare

We may think we can handle our nightmare but that is our cold logic speaking and not our hot emotional self. The emotional self-reacts automatically despite our best efforts. When our emotions are heightened, we can lose our calm self. While it may seem impossible to overcome, the solution that proved most effective was training. Our reactions are intrinsic, but the good news is just as in learning any physical skill muscle memory can be changed. Anticipating and practicing a different response to intense situations can change how you respond.

There is a 400-year-old model that can help create a new response to the sudden blindside hits. It can provide an override to your usual response as you shift the attention back to the other person and away from you. And in the process, you can help them find the best solution and that is one that they find for themselves. And it all begins by asking them a question.

An open honest question.

Deep intentional listening can lead to deep connection. Deep connection can lead to transformation.

You have tools to do this already. Let me help you find your nightmare so you will be ready the next time when all the eyes are on you and the question is asked.

"What would you do?"

Trolls

As our boat glided under one of the many small bridges sprinkled over Minnesota's 10,000 lakes something bright and colorful caught my eye. Perched on a ledge were five little goofy troll dolls grinning down at us from a perch where someone placed them. Each of the trolls smiled out from under its own wildly colored hair.

I smiled back but then I remembered the other kind of scary troll that lived under the bridge and challenged the three goats in the tale of "Billy Goats Gruff." That stinky, creepy, hungry troll challenged each of the three goats as they approached to cross to the sweet grass on the other side of his bridge.

First the small goat and then the medium goat came to the bridge where the troll called out, "I'm going to eat you!!" The little guy said, "Wait for the next one. He's bigger than me!" The troll let him pass.

Next the medium one came, and the troll challenged his passage. "I'm going to eat you!!" "Wait for the next one. He's bigger than me!" The troll let him pass.

Finally, the third goat came but the troll was the one who was surprised by the large, angry goat that showed the troll that he was nobody's lunch.

Trolls are nasty and even today their namesakes, the internet trolls, post lies that agitate and distract us from seeing that maybe some things need to work differently in this world that has changed.

Making a change in life is like crossing a bridge. Just that thought of change can overwhelm us, so it is hard to take the first step let alone make it to the other side. At any point we can turn around and go back. It is a matter of choice.

The goal is to make it across the bridge and if we anticipate the obstacles then we may be better prepared to overcome them.

Often the greatest obstacles are the ones we create for ourselves:

- "I'm too old."
- "Can't teach an old dog new tricks."
- "I don't care."

When we face them, it is like facing the troll under the bridge.

As the billy goats taught us, there was a way around the troll but it's up to us to figure out how to do so. In a way, that part that is holding you back is your own troll, your own obstacle, as it finds excuses not to even try.

If you are ready to make some changes here are some things to consider as you examine your personal trolls.

1. If you don't make a change, what will your life be like next year? Five years? Ten years?
2. Are you willing to do the work?
3. Are you ready to face the consequences for change?

Consider where you have been, where you are now and, most importantly, where you want to be.

You have the power to undertake this journey and facing the troll's challenge is the first step.

How we respond to the challenges of change affects how we survive. Resilience, rebounding in the face of adversity, is the key.

Finding the strength within can keep us going and facing your troll is a good place to start.

Reluctant Vision

"Why did that lady steal her dog?"

I looked down at my 4-year-old-granddaughter and tried to figure out what she was talking about.

It was a bright, hot morning and my granddaughter wanted to go for a walk through the neighborhood. Her goal was to show me her favorite house, her treasure, and her excitement was contagious.

She skipped her way to the end of her street and quickly disappeared around the corner. I scrambled to keep up with her.

As I turned the corner I spoke briefly to the neighbor and her dog as she watered her flowers. We smiled and waved and commented on the beautiful day. Her small dog was beside her as her vigilant companion.

Once again, my granddaughter ran ahead and then came back to me. "Come on! Can't you walk any faster?"

Just then I noticed a young woman jogger passing us. The neighbor's dog was following her, and the runner slowed to tell the dog to go back home. Reluctantly the dog turned back and was welcomed home by its owner.

We reached the special house and after a thorough inspection we retraced our steps. After we passed the neighbor and her dog my granddaughter stopped and pulled me aside to whisper a question.

"Why did that lady steal her dog?"

What? I was confused. I asked her to repeat her question.

Earnest little eyes looked up at me. "Why did that lady steal her dog?"

It took me a minute to unravel the four-year old's thread of thinking. In her rush to get to the special house she must not have noticed the neighbor's dog when we first passed by. She only saw the dog as it ran joyfully behind the jogger. She didn't notice the runner sending the dog home. She assumed they were together.

I tugged out her understanding. In my granddaughter's mind the jogger was running with her dog. When she saw it with the neighbor, she jumped to the conclusion that the neighbor 'stole' the runner's dog.

We stopped and I carefully went through each step of the scenario. I explained the neighbor, the dog and the jogger. The dog belonged to the neighbor lady. The dog was running with the jogger but didn't belong to her.

I was pleased at how logically I explained away her concerns. And instead of saying, "Oh, OK," she once again asked again in a way that reminded me that we were speaking different languages. To help me better understand her question she carefully enunciated the words,

"Why…did…that…lady…steal…her…dog?"

She had the story set in her mind and she wasn't going to give it up. This isn't just a four-year-old's mindset. I claim guilt as well.

A while back I was at the YMCA pool. I decided I would try water jogging and I stopped by where the flotation belts sit. There was a new bench, and I looked behind and around it, but I didn't see the belts. I went and asked the lifeguard, and she said, "They're over there by the bench."

I thought, "No. I already looked there, and I didn't see the belts." With a little irritation I went back and looked all over the ground. I did not see the belts.

I asked the guard again.

"They must be right under my nose, but I promise you I don't see them."

The guard said, "Look up. They're on the wall."

And there they were. If I had raised my eyes to look two feet higher, I would have bumped them with my nose. That was a little embarrassing. I envisioned them as on the floor as they had always been and I was determined to find them where I expected them to be.

We see what we expect to see and so many times we hear what we expect to hear. And when it doesn't fill our expectations there is dissonance between the two.

How many times have you heard this exchange?

Me: "Hello. How are you today?"

Karen: "Fine."

How would you react if the conversation went this way?

Me: "Hello. How are you today?"

Karen: "Oh I'm so glad you asked! The water heater broke and flooded my basement. The door fell off the refrigerator and landed on my foot."

The second conversation isn't what we expect to hear because it isn't following the standard script. Actually, it may be a little unsettling because we don't know what to expect next or how to respond.

Our minds have a filter through which we experience life. Those filters are created by our knowledge, experience, and culture. When we challenge our standard expectations, the brain struggles to reclaim its familiar footing.

Questioning our expectations can be a real challenge. First, they are part of who we are, and they determine our field of vision. We could call them "our truth" because expectation shapes our frame of reference. They don't come into question because they are an inherent part of who we are.

Secondly, once acknowledged, thinking in a different way is work. It's much easier to not apply patience and commitment and just do things as we always have. Like putting on a new pair of shoes, it takes effort because we're battling our own habits.

However, if we can push ourselves a bit and replace assumptions and expectations with a new perspective, our field of vision expands. If we can lift our eyes, even a degree or two a whole new world can emerge right before our eyes.

I would like to say that my careful, logical explanation of what occurred with the dog brought clear understanding. Instead, I received a very skeptical 4-year-old look.

And what happened next? When we got home, she ran into the house and said, "Mom, we just saw somebody steal a dog!!"

Bridging the Gap

THE ALARM on my phone rang. I reached for it. As I did, a fresh understanding came to me of the figurative phrase, "I feel like I've been runover by a MAC truck." I was stiff and hurt and since I forgot the hose to my CPAP machine, I was pretty sure I hadn't slept very well.

My mind jumped back to review the previous day. Almost right away I realized that the pain I felt wasn't just physical. There was a lot more involved than just some muscle and tissue. My mind and heart were hurting too.

My emotions had gotten the better of me and now I was suffering the consequences.

My trigger hit me at a national convention for professional speakers. I have years of preaching experience but now I was entering the secular world of professional speaking. I needed to catch the current trends, and this was the place to learn them.

I still considered myself a bit of a hermit following the lockdown. A convention filled with happy, excited people was a challenge for me to attend. I was never the one who drank and put a lampshade on my head at parties but usually I can hang in and have a good time. This day, however, was different. I was operating on a whole other tier of engagement that I had no idea was present.

It all began when I stepped into Opryland Hotel for the first time in over twenty-five years. That hotel and I have history.

James, the one I hold responsible for making me a widow, was a bellman at Opryland decades ago. The company provided good benefits including free counseling services for employees and spouses. The counseling offices were in a set of unassuming trailers at the back of the parking lot.

James and I had been married thirteen years at that point, but we began our new life together in those trailers. It was there that James uttered the life altering statement, "I think I may have developed a drinking problem." That was on a Tuesday. On Friday he was checking into rehab at Baptist Hospital with the full support of his supervisor. Opryland was good to us. Even years later when he answered the call to ministry, he continued to work there as he attended seminary.

If this rehab was going to work, I had my own clutter to work out too. Those trailers provided a healing place for me as well as I wrestled with my own set of challenges.

The hotel then was half its current size, and it was complete with an extravagant theme park in its own backyard. Sometimes, I would bring our young sons to see their daddy at work and he'd slip them away to buy them a Coca-Cola. Then they ran through the courtyard jungles and splashed in the fountains. One time my parents stayed there and my father, the traveling salesman, declared it to be a mighty fine hotel.

Yes. That hotel and I have history.

I planned to combine convention business with a family visit since my husband's brother lives nearby. I arrived in Nashville a day early so that I could get settled and have a good visit before I disappeared into the glamourous convention life for three days. That night the family and I shared a lot of memories about James. It was a good evening.

The next morning, I woke at 5:00 am to get to the hotel to meet a supportive friend for breakfast. She knew this was my first time to come to this meeting and she had kindly offered to show me the ropes.

The day was Saturday and even with no traffic at that early hour there was a portent of the day.

The GPS gave me three route choices. Nothing seemed simple. Parking was harder than I remembered. I forgot to download a map of the hotel, and the walk was much further than I expected. The unknown made me edgy.

I entered the lobby from a side door that led directly into the thick jungle of plants where my sons once played. Without a transitional space like the lobby the wave of emotions almost took my breath away. Memories of my husband, my family, and that critical time of healing my life spilled from my heart. A whole crucible of emotions bubbled up from some deep place and nearly swept me away.

I pushed ahead.

At the convention's reception desk, I received my name tag. I looked around and didn't recognize anyone. Once again, I pushed ahead as I made myself walk up to complete strangers and introduce myself.

Everyone was friendly. I met my friend for breakfast and that was a relief. Then throughout the day the other attendees and I exchanged business cards and, in the hustle and bustle I made commitments without a good idea of where any place was or how long it would take to get there.

"Meet for dinner at the mall next door?" "Sure! Count me in!"

"Can you come to the ice cream social later?" "Sure! I'd love to!"

What I didn't take into consideration was that everything was on foot and there was a whole lot of walking. Walking takes time. I had in over 6,000 steps and it wasn't even noon!

There were breakout sessions and general meetings. The information was great. The food was delicious. As the day wore on, however, I began longing for just a quiet spot where I could pause and regroup. I was deeply tired, and it was barely halfway through the day.

Onward I pushed myself. There was more delicious food and then more people to meet and more information to learn and… and… I was beginning to feel overwhelmed. And since I wasn't staying at the hotel there were limited places to sit and rest to collect oneself.

I hit the wall. As the saying goes, I found my last nerve.

The last big meeting of the day was in a very large ballroom packed with tables, bright pulsing lights, a big stage and lots and lots of extroverts. The meeting began with a half dozen drummers marching as if leading a parade. All around me were people smiling and applauding all there was to celebrate. We applauded everyone's accomplishments. We applauded each speaker. We applauded the touching memorial video of the members who had died.

I was ready to go home. The meeting wasn't the problem. I was.

The stress from my people pleasing was wearing me out. Not once that day had I said "no" to anything. Of all the people I worried about pleasing nowhere was I on the list. And like in the story about the comedienne who took a stranger to get cash from her ATM, my strong emotions disconnected me from logic. I was on autopilot and the plane was going down.

What could I do? I had found some friends and now I was sitting in the middle of a very large ballroom with my book coach, my publisher and two of their friends. I didn't just want to get up and leave. That didn't seem polite.

When the drums began playing again, I screwed up my courage. I said my good-byes to those at my table and found my way to the door. That metal click of pushing the release bar and the cool whoosh of the air in the lobby was very satisfying.

But I was stubborn. I made a commitment, and this autopilot wasn't about to give up. From the hotel I walked the long distance to the restaurant where I would meet up with members of my organization's local chapter. How many steps at that point? I was too exhausted to look, and I probably didn't want to know anyway especially when it began to softly rain.

It was a German restaurant with terrible service and when the throbbing in my head matched the beat of the om-pah band I began to believe that I had gone a bridge too far. Finally, common sense wiggled its way to the surface, and I texted the hostess of the ice cream social. I was too beat to go any further.

Luckily, someone at dinner gave me a ride to my car. It was almost 10:00 pm by the time I reached my brother-in-law's house. It had been a 17-hour day. I sat in the car. That walk from the driveway to the house felt like it was another 6,000 steps even though it was only a few feet away. I got there though and fell into bed. It felt so good.

It was the next morning when I realized just how stiff and tired, I was from the day before. I lay in the bed garnering my strength to make it to day two of the convention when something finally got through my thick head.

I didn't take care of myself because I was unaware of what I was doing. Logic clicked off. I was totally emotional. In the process, I forgot about taking care of myself. No. I didn't just forget to use self-care. The idea didn't even come to my mind.

Throughout the long hard stretch of the day before, I did none of the things I advise people to do when they are stressed out, exhausted and at the end of their rope. No, just like that comedienne who took the sketchy stranger with her to her ATM, I zoned out.

- I started the day tired and didn't provide for breaks
- I didn't fully engage the day but stayed just a bit agitated.
- I overcommitted based on my lack of information.

- I didn't listen to my body but continued to push through fatigue.
- I picked up the energy and forgot to regulate my own.
- I forgot to breathe.

The combination of feeling anxious about attending a national meeting at my husband's old hotel, a hotel filled with memories and was an essential part of our healing, combined to become a zone of overwhelm even before I reached the registration desk.

My emotions got the better of me. My logic never had a chance. I was on emotional autopilot, and, in the process, I lost myself completely.

How does one overcome an automatic response? According to the studies cited in the podcast the most effective solution was training. We can learn a different response. And the good news is that just as in any skill, muscle memory can be changed.

The pilot of the US Airways jet that landed in the icy waters of the Hudson River in 2009 attributed the success not his personal skill but to the years of training that he and all the crew members completed. They had their own version of autopilot that took over and resulted in no loss of life.

How does that work in the everyday world?

One way to create a new response to sudden life questions is through use of a 400-year-old Listening Method. Intentional listening can help create an override to your usual response as you shift the attention away from yourself to the other person. With you out of the way, you can help them find the best solution: the one that they find for themselves.

It all begins by asking a question.

Once I realized what transpired the day before, I was embarrassed and began beating up on myself. That wasn't helping either. So, I resolved to make this day better.

- I intentionally took my time going in.
- I intentionally skirted the edges of the meeting.
- I intentionally engaged in some less frantic card-exchanging conversations.
- I intentionally breathed to center myself in the middle of everyone else's energy.

When I felt myself tense up, I breathed. When I was tired, I sat down on one of the benches. My awareness of what happened the day before was the first step to make this day better.

Nothing I did was flashy, but it was effective, nonetheless. At the end of day two, I was much less tired. And one thing is certain. My feet were much happier as I definitely walked much fewer steps.

Umbrellas of Wellbeing
SUDDEN CHANCE OF RAIN

I SAT in the car hoping the downpour would end soon. The rain was one of those sudden summer showers that weather channels caution about. One minute the sky was a crystal-clear blue, and the next the wind was buffeting the car, and the drains in the parking lot backed up with water coming too fast to accommodate the flow.

The local college was sponsoring a program on mental health. As I waited in my car for the rain to let up, I watched several people making their way to the entrance. Each carried an open umbrella of a different color. The solid colors were the most popular. Red and black ones were the standard choices. I saw a pink one, and another that was blue with big butterflies. A large green and white golf umbrella stood out boldly against the others.

I held my bright, garden-themed umbrella in my lap as I was poised to make a run for the entrance. As the wind pushed against my door, I pulled the handle, slid out of the car, and opened my umbrella.

The fabric canopy unfurled as I pressed the button on the shaft. Just as I felt that satisfying click that locks the umbrella in its open position, a gust of wind caught it. The frame and its canopy were pushed beyond their limits. Suddenly my umbrella was broken and useless against the rain.

I ran through the rain to the library door and pushed through to the lobby still holding my broken umbrella. The other umbrellas were neatly stored in a rack to dry. With only their handles showing, they looked far more alike than before. The individual colors were hidden in the rack so that only a uniform row of handles poked above the stand.

I laid my broken umbrella on the floor beside the rack. My handle and the exposed framework looked like theirs, but it was battered and most likely terminally ill. The once pretty fabric canopy was now inside out, showing only a pale version of its inner side.

The Body and Its Canopy

Mental health was the symposium topic that brought me to this place. Like so many others I thought I had a pretty good idea of what mental health entailed.

As I looked at my broken umbrella, though, I had a shift in perspective. My once vital umbrella was now sick. Was there a way to make it better? My experience told me most likely no, but now I realized that personal experience was also coloring my understanding of mental health. I realized my attitude toward mental health was limited to my experience of watching my brother battle mental illness his whole life.

Somehow, like many, I equivocated mental health only with mental illness. I needed to move past that limited understanding and look at mental health in a broader way.

As I remembered the different umbrellas open over their owners, I realized that much like those multi-colored canopies, mental health is an umbrella that is a part of our overall health.

The whole framework, from the handle to the ribs that anchor the fabric canopy, is like our physical health. Every human arrives on this earth with the same physical equipment, like bones, blood, and organs. When the physical framework isn't working optimally, we seek some kind of care.

If the frame represents our physical self, we could say mental health is like the fabric canopy over our heads. It's connected to the physical frame. Its pie shaped pieces are like the many facets of who we are.

Like the umbrellas that paraded by my car, each was different in appearance but the same in substance. Yes, we are physical beings, but the parts of who we are individually appear here through our social, emotional, and spiritual needs and expectations. Just like those colors I saw from the individual umbrellas, each of us is unique and shaped by outside forces such as our culture and background.

A Spring's Tension

The critical part of the umbrellas is something that doesn't even show. Inside the central stick is a long spring that moves as the umbrella opens and closes. The spring tightens to hold the canopy in place with tension until the runner clicks in place at the top. The tension is released as the runner brings the canopy back down to the handle. The wind gust took my umbrella past the tension point and broke the spring inside.

This also describes people when they have lost the healthy balance between physical health and mental health. Seeking help for physical problems is widely acceptable, but when we feel totally stripped out emotionally, then there is often cultural stigma against seeking help. Normally we connect the idea of preventative medicine to physical health, but it is also essential to mental health. Small problems addressed up front often prevent more serious ones later.

UMBRELLAS OF WELLBEING

All Parts Together

It is well documented that physical health and mental health go hand in hand. Studies show that worry can create a stomachache. Low blood sugar can bring on anxiety. Addressing one problem can bring relief to another.

In his book, *When the Body Says No*, Gabor Mate, MD, explores the stress/disease connection as each of us struggles to navigate daily life. Even our environment impacts our health.

The term mental *well-being* would be a better expression of what mental health fully entails. Well-being covers how you manage your life in the face of challenging situations. It includes how you feel about yourself, your connection with others, and the way you manage that tension or stress, all of which can affect your physical health.

Mental well-being is about balancing the social, emotional, and spiritual facets of our lives. Just like the physical health/mental health connection, we are a balance of the handle, the shaft, the framework, and the beautiful fabric canopy of those umbrellas. Each component needs the other to work its best.

All of us have our rainstorms. Much like the drains in the parking lot, we can usually handle what comes, but sometimes life's difficulties arrive fast and furious. It's at those times that mental well-being can sustain us as we ride out the storm.

So, the next time the rains come, what does your umbrella look like?

PART V

Heart to Heart: The Journey to Deep Listening
LISTENING

Mountains of Expectations

"Daggone it," I thought. Here I was on a lifetime adventure and the clouds blocked my view.

I was flying from Rome to Munich as my 2019 dream vacation ended and I was headed home to the United States. In anticipation of a bird's eye view of the Alps I even paid extra for a window seat. The day was clear and beautiful as I continued to scan the horizon for a glimpse of what I hoped to see. Just as we reached the base of the mountain range, thick clouds elbowed their way into the landscape and blocked the view below.

Clouds hold no nationality. I can see those at home. Just as I began to turn away in disappointment something caught my eye. The white mountain peaks had been there. They were so tall that they poked their way *through* the clouds. I just didn't recognize them because they weren't the stony rock mountains I was expecting. Even in July they were covered with so much snow that the craggy white mountain tops blended with the cloud cover and appeared like ice floats on an arctic sea.

MOUNTAINS OF EXPECTATIONS

I don't know what my expectations were. Perhaps I thought there would be some big hills with a little snow on top of them. What I saw was so majestic it literally took my breath away. The snow caps sparkled above the brilliantly white clouds, and it was difficult to get my mind around what I was seeing. It was hard to accept it for the beautiful gift it was. My mind wrestled to file this incredible view into a familiar context but there was none. This was completely new.

Soon we landed and I mulled over what I had just seen. I almost missed an indescribably beautiful view because I didn't understand the possibilities beyond my own limited experience with real mountains. I was expecting something like the background of the movie "The Sound of Music." What I got was so much more.

That flight came to mind as I watched my handyman wrestling to assemble a disappointingly flimsy storage shed that looked so much better online but came with half of its parts missing. Once again, I questioned how many times my expectation has been out of sync with reality. How many times was I disappointed over an unfulfilled expectation and then got mad when it didn't go as I planned? Too many.

Those moments can be tough, but it can go the other way as well. Sometimes expectations are met beyond measure.

I saw this over and over again with my husband James' illness. He was facing incredibly difficult odds. Yet I thought I knew what I needed to know. After all, I was a critical care hospital chaplain. I worked with hospice patients and organ donor families. I taught the stages of grief to patients and family. Yet this situation was different. This was personal. I thought I had a handle on things but somehow just as I thought we'd reached a plateau, more bad news arrived at the doorstep.

Finally, it was when I got myself and my expectations out of the way that I experienced how God and the universe can work if we just let it.

We were moving to my home area because we needed help as James' condition continued to deteriorate. I was a board-certified chaplain with over 20 years of experience so it came as a surprise when I couldn't find a job where we needed to be. One hospital even flew me in for an interview and even though the position didn't feel like a good fit, I was surprised when I didn't even receive a job offer.

We were at a crossroad. James was about to try another approach in his care, and we needed to either push ahead and make the move or stay put.

One morning on my drive to the hospital I was stewing over possible outcomes. Feeling a little desperate I said out loud, "Lord, I'm happiest when I'm serving you!" I was alone in the car so if anybody heard it had to be somebody on the other side of the veil that separates our world and the much larger world of spirit.

The response I heard with my heart was, "Think outside the box."

As I entered the office, I was surprised to see the liaison for LOPA (Louisiana Organ Procurement Agency) visiting my director. I recognized her from organ donor cases I had worked on over the years.

A lightbulb went off in my head. "Think outside the box." While she met with my director, I turned on my computer and searched for "organ donation" at my new location. Immediately a job opening appeared. It had been open for a while. Was this what I was looking for?

There would be no move without a job, but this certainly wasn't the one I had in mind.

The LOPA rep left, and I followed her down the hall. She smiled when she saw me, and I shared with her my dilemma. She said, "Of course, I would recommend you for the job. You've worked with us before."

I made the call to Kentucky Organ Donation Affiliates (KODA) and I was just the type of candidate they were looking for to support the families of organ donors. A phone call and then a quick trip home for an in-person interview, and the job was mine.

That was only the beginning. It was like the first domino hitting the next one in line. The progression began and as it did, each piece of the puzzle fell into place.

- My mother offered us her little rental house so we had a place to stay.
- We listed our house and it sold.
- An army of friends appeared and helped with the major downsize required in moving from a four-bedroom house to two-bedroom house.
- My brother-in-law packed and drove the moving truck.

The next step was James' care. Deciding the who, what, when, and where of moving a terminally ill cancer patient was daunting. We were moving home, though, so we had resources.

- Family stood ready to help.
- My mother's tenants had already given notice, so the rental house was available.
- The job's schedule was perfect for balancing James' care while maintaining full-time employment.

A lung cancer survivor friend who was active in cancer support groups suggested Dr. K, an oncologist specializing in lung issues. I called the cancer center with my heart pounding in my throat. I explained our situation.

"Is it possible to get an appointment with Dr. K?"

The question hung in the air like one of those slow-motion movies where the ball is tossed and slowly, slowly the tension is released when waiting hands first touch the ball.

"No problem," The oncologist's office replied. "That is called 'transfer of care.'"

I gave a deep sigh of relief. Tears of joy danced around the edges of my eyes.

But there was so much more. I continued to trust the process that was in motion. Over time, I realized that much like my expectations of my mountain view, my aim was way too low.

Remarkably, James' Mississippi college roommate now lived where we were moving. As we drove back to New Orleans from the job interview, I suggested that he call his friend to tell him that we would be there soon. I drove while James called. He shared the news and then asked how his wife Linda was doing.

"Oh, she retired from teaching. She now works at the Cancer Center. AND she shares an office with Dr. K's cancer navigator."

As in, Dr. K our new oncologist.

I almost drove off the road in shock. Then I laughed with joy. God was there already. Once again God provided the answer for a question that we didn't even know we had.

"Let go and let God."

How many times have we heard that one?

I know I've heard it plenty of times, but this is what my experience has shown me.

It's true.

Deep Listening

REMEMBER there is a difference between hearing and listening.

- Hearing is simply taking in sounds without necessarily any interpretation.
- Listening uses ears and your mind as you make meaning from what you heard.
- Deep listening is listening with the heart.

Our routines are basically habits, right? Doing things as we always do them can be as comfortable as slipping into a pair of old shoes. But a new pair of shoes draws your attention to your feet and makes you walk funny until you break them in, and they adapt to your stride.

Intentional listening can like that new pair of shoes. It can draw you in a different direction as you step out of your routine responses and communicate in a new way. Deep listening means listening with all of your senses and not just your ears.

Deep intentional listening tunes you into the true meaning that is hiding behind the words.

Transform is a fancy word for change. Maybe you are satisfied with where you are and how you listen. However, a study with experienced critical care nurses at a New Orleans area hospital revealed that even something as simple as asking a question can lead to change for both the nurse and the patient.

Are you ready?

It all begins with a question.

Crumbs

A SMALL STEAM room at the local YMCA might be an odd place for an informal counseling session, but there's something about the hazy, quiet atmosphere that helps people relax and open up.

People talk. I listen. That's what I do.

Invitations

The fairy tale *Hansel and Gretel* tells the story of a brother and a sister lost in the woods. Gretel is clever and leaves a trail of breadcrumbs to mark the way home. What she didn't know was that crumbs aren't just bits of bread or crackers. Crumbs can also be an invitation.

Unfortunately for the children, the birds did what birds do. They gobbled up the crumbs as fast as they were laid down!

Have you ever sat and fed pigeons at a park? At first, birds will watch from a distance. Toss a few crumbs for a single bird and suddenly the whole flock descends. Any movement will scare them back to their safe spot, but they continue to watch and hope for more.

CRUMBS

The crumbs are an invitation for the birds to come and engage. They are a form of communication.

Crumbs come in other forms too.

Steam Room Conversations

After my water exercise class, everybody heads for the steam room to warm up after being in the cold pool. We say that's our reason, but it's really a time to gather and share before we step back into the cold world of everyday life.

Sometimes I stay a bit longer in the steam. These brief moments of solitude give me a minute to say a little prayer or simply plan my day.

On this day, a large, muscular man sat in the steam room. Not too close and not too far away. The steam dissipated and details emerged. He was a very fit man in his 70s.

I was just about to leave when he arrived. A conversation quickly began. As I mentioned, people talk, and I listen.

The man, John, said he retired as an Emergency Medical Technician (EMT). He told me about the deep slump that followed his retirement. It was tough, but his wife and friends didn't let him give up.

Now, he was on a mission to help other EMTs suffering from the trauma they see and feel daily.

He was focused on his training for a bicycle fundraiser for military dogs.

As I began asking more questions, the heat from the steam room hit me. My body reached its limit, and I needed to leave. I gave a quick goodbye and left. The sharp, cool air around the pool provided instant relief.

A sip of cool water restored me a bit, but another part of me didn't feel quite right. Somehow the conversation with John didn't exactly feel finished.

The unfinished conversation nagged me throughout the day. I repeatedly ran it over in my mind. Why did it feel so incomplete?

Deeper Signals

The answer came that evening as I sliced crumbly cornbread for dinner.

John dropped crumbs for me. Those crumbs were words slipped into the seemingly normal conversation. They reflected a need to speak of something deeper. The words "depression," "trauma," "mission," and "SEALS" … had he been a Navy SEAL?

I thought of the few patients over the years who trusted me with memories of near-death experiences. They had a need to tell their tale and process it, a need to understand their experience. These were life-changing events not to be trusted to just anyone. Could they trust me with their story?

For one patient, the crumb was an offhand remark about an out of body experience, seeing himself lying in the hospital bed, I encouraged him to continue. "Then I heard a sound that was green."

I passed this patient's loyalty test. He went on sharing his experience. He was given a choice to stay over on the other side or return to fight his way back to health. The thought of the special-ed students he taught instantly brought him back into his very sick body.

Love. Love brought him back. Love was the thread weaving through the stories of return and recovery that were shared with me.

Deeper Connection

A listening study I led with critical care nurses showed us that when you listen, really listen, deep things happen.

Deep listening leads to connection. Connection leads to transformation.

What is transformation? Change. Maybe it's a quiet rumble. Maybe it's a massive, tectonic shake. Either way, it's a noticeable shift. That's why listening is so important. Change can happen for you as the listener and for the individual telling their story.

To the man in the steam room, I apologize. You wanted to trust me with your story, and I let you down. I was getting too hot. I couldn't stay any longer.

I had hoped to see you again, but I haven't. Those moments of trust and openness are so delicate and precious that they rarely occur twice.

So, when somebody tosses you a crumb, grab it. Accept this incredible gift of connection. That's what's important. That's why we do what we do. It's all about love.

That man in the steam room gave me a gift. I wasn't there for him. He was there for me. I needed to remember how important something as simple as a crumb can be.

Because people talk, I listen. That's what I do, and you can too.

Stray Friends

"THERE'S a stray dog on your deck blocking the door. He growled and won't let me get in to feed Miss Ruthie."

I was on vacation, packing for my return home, when my cat sitter sent the text.

"Miss Ruthie has plenty of food. Just wanted to let you know what you were walking into."

I'd been gone a week, and, while I was gone, a stray dog claimed my deck as his own. His breed wasn't known for friendliness, and it would be almost dark by the time I got home.

What was I going to do?

Believe me, I'm a dog lover. My hope is that, when I die, at least six of my favorite dogs will greet me in heaven with tails wagging.

The sitter's report, however, indicated this dog might have a different greeting for me.

During the six-hour drive home, I had time to mull things over. The dog had shown aggression, which limited my options. Children play in my neighborhood. People go for strolls on the levee behind my house. Other people could be affected.

I knew the animal control folks in my town to be good people. I knew they would do everything they could for him once they caught him. But the dog would need to be caught. That was the problem.

Mississippi Delta – 1990s

My mind wandered back to the 1990s, to the small Mississippi Delta town that adopted a stray black dog for a while. I pastored a church there and the postmistress of the tiny post office kept me up on the daily local news.

No one knew where the young black dog came from. The postmistress made sure he had the basics of food and water, but over time he charmed his way into the town's heart. He was delightful. He greeted every car but artfully dodged too much engagement. He wanted to play it his way and that didn't include submitting to any of us who would have loved to take him and provide a good home.

One dog-lover managed to coax him into her car and took him home, but it wasn't long before he was back ruling his post office kingdom. He was always friendly, but he never committed to a single person.

Fall came, and, as the weather got colder, something was obvious. No matter what we wanted for that dog, he set his own path.

January came and I headed north to Chicago for two weeks of school. Before I left, I saw the dog for what would be the last time. I said to him, "Just choose one of us. We all want to give you a good home." The dog, however, had his own agenda.

When I returned two weeks later the dog was gone and the postmistress said she didn't know what happened. Some hunters camped nearby, and he had hung around them. She hoped maybe one of them finally sweet talked him into going home with them.

I felt pretty sad. The lack of closure was unsettling.

For quite a while I continued to look for him. My eyes searched the woods near the road where the campers had been. I even kept an eye on the edge of the road to see if he had been hit and killed by a passing car, but there was no resolution. He was simply gone.

I wondered if the dog waiting on my deck would be the same.

Home – Present Day

When I pulled into my driveway, the dog suddenly came from behind the bushes, not to rush at me, but to run away. I startled him. I felt compassion rather than fear as I saw the ribs of such a tough dog.

How did he come to be here? How did he come to choose my home? Did somebody abandon him?

A part of me hoped he would be gone, and another part, my heart, *wanted to help*.

He ran to the levee and from a distance I saw him cautiously watching me.

I pulled together some scraps to make a little meal.

I couldn't give the dog a home, but I could try to help. If nothing else maybe, like that Mississippi dog, all I could do was give him a place to rest before he goes on the next leg of his journey.

I set the food out and went into the house. As if by magic, the food and the dog disappeared.

The food I placed out the night before was gone too, so I called the good folks at animal control. They would have the best chance of either reuniting him with his owners or finding him a good home. That was my dream for him.

But, maybe like that Mississippi dog, this dog had other plans.

Regardless of Results

I'm reminded of people I've tried to help in the past. Usually there's been some kind of plan, either mine or theirs. Sometimes the help ended well, and sometimes it didn't. Sometimes the outcome is unpredictable.

Sometimes we are not responsible for the fix. Sometimes just being present with someone who is lost or suffering is all we are called to do.

I haven't seen the dog since last Friday. The cage to catch him sits in my yard as an invitation to a new life. It's an invitation and not a command. I hope he comes back but if he doesn't, I'm ok with that.

I gave it my best shot. That's all I'm asked to do.

Trilobite
CAIRN

A CAIRN IS a man-made stack of rocks memorializing a particular event. Jacob placed one to follow his dream of God. In other countries, such as Scotland, a stack of stones serves as a marker along a path, guiding the way ahead.

That's what happened to me. An unusual stone took me on a different path.

My stone was a trilobite, a fossil that peered back at me through the microscope in my college geology class. To most, it would've been just another rock, but that day, as I examined it more closely under a microscope, the image of the prehistoric animal revealed itself. Like a true cairn, it showed me that I was headed in the wrong direction.

Geology

I first fell in love with physical geology through an introductory class in my freshman year. Throughout the semester each class brought new, practical knowledge that I could associate with the hills, rocks, and water that I passed every day.

What I learned was practical, vital knowledge. What made it even more special was that my geologist professor shared his love for his work, and his enthusiasm helped me love it too.

I understand why I now remember so little about the next geology class I took. I expected it to be like the first class that I loved.

The second class was about fossils and where to find oil. To me those topics were as dry and boring as the professor, and I realized that if I were to make the best of this, I needed a plan. Gradually, I made one. I was already in the earliest possible class.

Step two was to go to class every single time and take plenty of notes. Finally, the essential step was to stay up all night before the test and review, review, and review my notes again. Then without going to bed, I immediately ran to the test location to spill out every single bit of knowledge that was temporarily housed in my short-term memory.

I don't remember my final grade but somehow, I passed. What was even more amazing was that, despite my painful study methods, I decided geology was the path for me.

My Personal Cairn was a Trilobite

I almost immediately met the trilobite in my third class. That trilobite became my cairn, and it was telling me that I was not on the right path.

Almost immediately, I could see that my poor excuse for studying that got me through the last class wasn't going to work for this one. In the previous class, I could rely on snippets of hastily 'learned' information to pass the test.

For this third class, I needed to engage the material and let it wiggle its way into me so that I wasn't merely someone who took a geology class. I needed to embrace it, like the first professor whose love for his work helped cement the course's knowledge, transferring from the master to the novice.

Knowing by Heart

I needed to let it change me as I embraced a whole body of knowledge. If I were to succeed, I needed to learn that knowledge by heart.

How do we know something by heart? Something comes to you without you even looking for it. It's more than simple repetition.

As you embrace knowledge, it embraces you. Over time, it works its way into your heart and soul, prepared to step forth whenever needed. And when it comes, it's an authentic expression.

For the musician, it makes the difference between a mediocre replaying of notes on a page and being genuinely moved by what's played. For the athlete, it's performing a particular movement perfectly, without even being aware.

This type of knowledge is heart-centered, and heart knowledge resonates with the truth inside us.

It tucks itself away until it's needed. Then, like the deep-sea diver rising through the water to reach the surface, it makes itself known.

Sand

I thought about heart knowledge the other day in my water fitness class.

Someone asked what I would speak on at my next engagement. I planned to talk about how God's love clings to us despite ourselves, so I gave a single word and response, "sand."

Just hearing that one word, without any further explanation on my part, half a dozen women simultaneously broke into the same exact song that was tucked away, a song they learned decades earlier as children. Even as children, they knew the wisdom of the lyrics.

"A wise man builds his house upon a rock," and "a foolish man builds his house upon the sand."

They knew even then that the foolish man would lose everything in the first big storm that blew his way.

That core theme was impressed upon their hearts. Yet when they stopped to remember the rest of the song, the words never came.

It was the essence of the song, its wisdom, that remained with them through all these years, waiting for its time to speak.

Welcoming the Heart's Wisdom

Head smarts have their place. They're like my information dump for my geology test—not always around for the long haul!

The type of understanding that lasts belongs to those who, like my first professor, love what they do and act from the heart.

Heart knowledge burrows deep within our psyche, bonding and staying dormant until it needs to be shared. This knowledge is a heart connection. It brings a richer, fuller life whether it is in the classroom, the boardroom, or the dining room.

Each of us, in some deep place within, holds a song of wisdom longing to be remembered and heard.

Rest assured that it will spring forth just when it's needed.

Ask. Invite. Welcome that wisdom of the heart.

PART VI

Taking the Plunge
ACTION

Grounding 5, 4, 3, 2, 1
IT STARTED WITH A SLEEPLESS NIGHT

THE OTHER NIGHT was a restless one. I'm not sure if it was the jolt of caffeine late in the day or if I simply wasn't tired enough. I turned from one side to another and couldn't get comfortable.

Eventually, I gave up on sleep. I climbed out of the bed and made my way to the kitchen to make some soothing tea. The teakettle was soon whistling. I watched the brewing tea grow stronger and stronger. I was careful not to let it brew too long. Just as I was aware of the time that called me to bed, I was keenly aware that the clock would soon be speaking to me. This time it would designate a new day whether I was ready or not.

The tea did its job, and I finally relaxed enough to doze off. As it turned out, I slept too well! In a flash, my alarm called me back from the land of Nod. Even then, my body declined the invitation.

I hit the snooze button once, twice, and on the third round of buzzing, I struggled to step back into the physical world. After two cups of strong coffee, I still felt out of sync with my body.

If I didn't have plans with someone, I would have surrendered to the siren call of my bed. The room was cool. My bed was warm. No. Going back to bed was not an option.

I fussed a bit with myself. I advise people about such things as self-care, and, suddenly, I was wrestling with my own basic principles.

I got dressed and carefully made my way down the icy steps to the car. The windshield was frosted over and the thought of scraping it clean made me groan. My mind was like an old cranky school bus that decided to be a little stubborn on this cold morning.

I started the engine to warm the car and set the defrost to full blast. If I sat there long enough, would the frost clear itself? Some may call it magical thinking, but at that moment it was the best I could negotiate with myself.

I let out a heavy yawn. If I didn't wake up and grasp the moment, what lay ahead of me was a very long day.

How can I fully wake up? How can I align my mind and my body?

Then understanding flooded over me. *This is what it means to ground oneself.* I had awoken in the middle of a dream, and it was as if a part of me was still there. I needed to bring the real, physical me and my dream me back together.

Common Knowledge, Essential Wisdom

In the weeks leading up to this sleepless night, I came across a notebook from a long-ago workshop. In the margin, I'd drawn an arrow to advice that was by now long forgotten.

"Grounding is remembering who you are in your physical space. It is getting out of the whirling mind and refocusing on the body." A Google search reveals this idea to be common knowledge, but on a morning like this, I needed to remember this basic wisdom.

Clare Biedenharn, DMin, BCC

One way I like to ground myself when I'm feeling out of sorts is to stop and stand in my space. It might be my physical space or maybe just a quiet mind. When I do, I imagine my feet first as standing solid on the ground. Then, in my mind's eye, my feet become like tree roots growing deeper and deeper. When I feel solid in my attachment to the Earth, I know I can take whatever storms may blow my way.

A Method of Grounding

I sat in the slowly warming car with my eyes closed. When I opened them, there was a clear patch on the windshield.

I wasn't ready to get back out of the car and try the ice scraper. I would wait a bit longer.

I closed my eyes again as something else came to mind. I read another piece of classic advice on grounding. This memory at that moment was a gift. A method of grounding.

To start, open your eyes and begin and think of the descending numbers 5, 4, 3, 2, 1.

- 5. Look around at five physical things you can see:
- I looked at the car's dashboard, the frosted windshield, the bush beside my car, my cup in the holder, and the pink pen on the floor beside my feet.

- 4. Touch 4 things:
- I touched the cold steering wheel, my scarf, the dashboard clock, and my glasses on the seat beside me.

- 3. Listen for three things outside of yourself:
- The motor hummed. The defroster blew air against the windshield. The back windshield wiper swooshed.

GROUNDING 5, 4, 3, 2, 1

- 2. Smell 2 Smells:
- I smelled my coffee and then realized that my car still had just a hint of its new car smell.

- 1. Taste 1 thing:
- I lifted my cup and tasted the still warm coffee.

By now, the clear patch on the windshield was almost complete, and what was left would easily be swept away by the wipers. Just those few moments not only brought me peace but helped me dodge the dreaded ice scraper.

It was still cold outside but somehow, I felt connected with myself. I felt fully in my body and my mind felt clearer.

There was no big dramatic change for me in just those few moments, but I felt better. I no longer felt that a part of me was still cozily wrapped in flannel sheets in a dream world. I was in the moment. Even though the shift was slight, those few moments changed the rest of the day.

5, 4, 3, 2, 1 made for an easy liftoff.

Timeline

I ALWAYS DID WELL in school except when it came to one big roadblock. On my report card my history grade was always high. My math grade was…well, let's say on the other end of the scale. The one thing that saved me from total loss came the day that I realized a number line was just another version of a timeline.

In each instance there is a line and there is a midpoint located on that line. In math that's usually designated as 'zero.' Go in one direction, there are negative numbers. Look in the other direction and there are positive numbers. Zero is right in the middle.

It's not so different with a timeline.

Imagine standing on a line painted on the ground; let's call it your personal timeline. Pick one direction and call it your past. The other direction is your future. The midpoint, ground zero, is where you are standing now, and it is the only part of life that you have immediate control over. The present moment is the 'right now' of your life.

The past is over and done with. We can remember the past, but we can't change it. If you have a painful memory, it is an event stuck in time and each time you remember it, you are bringing it into the present and experiencing it all over again. But it will always have the same outcome. You don't get resolution. You get a fresh shot of pain. Like the movie "Groundhog Day," where every day is exactly like the one before. Despite the best intentions, the past can't be changed.

Let it go.

The future lies ahead and while your current decisions may affect your future, it is still unfolding. You are not there yet. So, just like we can't live in the past, we can't live in the future either. We don't always know what's coming but that doesn't mean we don't have power over what it may be. We are not victims. We have choices through our decisions that help shape our outcomes.

What we live in is the 'right now.' Our peace lies there because from moment to moment, it is all that we have. It is what is true in life. The present moment, this mindfulness, is with you always and it is one thing you can control. It is the one place where life can be fully lived. Right here and now is the present moment.

You can change the course of your future by making changes NOW. A tweak here. A tweak there. Little things can make big changes. Let's say you're on a ship leaving South America headed for Japan. If that ship's compass is off just a degree or two at the beginning, the error compounds as you proceed across the Pacific Ocean and you will find yourself in Hong Kong or Malaysia. A slight adjustment at the beginning of the voyage could have kept you on course to land where you intended to be.

Right now, as you stand between your past and future, consider this. If your present moment shapes your future, then what is your trajectory? Where are you headed personally or professionally? Where do you want to be five, ten, or twenty years from now? If you don't like what you see coming, you have the power to change NOW. Your NOW decisions will shape the outcome.

Small changes can have big effects. Ask yourself, "What am I willing to do to be a part of the solution and not stay anchored in the problem?"

Claim your personal timeline. Acknowledge the past. Forgive what you can because hard feelings will only hold you down. Look to the future. What's the vision you have for yourself?

We live in dynamic times, so it is important to get a handle on things and decide what you need to do or change to create the future you want.

The future begins now. It begins with a dream for yourself and acceptance that wishes can come true.

It happens one decision at a time.

Ancestor Trees

LAST YEAR my sister and I went to a celebration of our childhood neighborhood. When we were growing up the houses there were just considered old. This event was to celebrate our old stomping grounds as a designated historic street. A neighborhood built as part of a stately development at the end of a streetcar line that climbed its way up to the new homes.

Mature oaks and maples lined our street and turned beautiful shades of gold and yellow as one season closed, and another began. As a child I never thought about how those trees got there but then at the celebration I saw an old, scratchy, sepia-toned picture of our home when it was first built. It took me a minute to even recognize it as the house I called home. In my eyes, the faded picture showed a house that was bare. Perched upon an empty hill, that image reminded me of some spanking new subdivisions built atop a recently plowed cornfield.

It was odd to see our bare-naked house. The edges were so sharp it was almost painful to see. I couldn't help but look away. This was still a new raw looking house. It had not yet gained the warm patina of home shaped by generations of children, pets and plantings.

ANCESTOR TREES

Who planted the trees that now provide cool breezes and shade? How did they come to be?

Were they carefully, thoughtfully planted or did they volunteer like the backyard persimmon tree that my mother continued to mourn after the utility company cut it down?

In families, the people who came before you are your ancestors. Your mother and father had parents, and they were your grandparents. Those grandparents had parents and grandparents and the line from which you come goes back a long, long way. You may not know their names, but they are still a part of your lineage. Their DNA became yours. The unnamed are a part of who you are.

Who planted the trees in my old yard? I'll never know but I thank them. Those unnamed are like my ancestors. We may not share DNA, but I was blessed by their vision. Those unnamed followed through on a dream for the neighborhood that made my street beautiful. It was someone's vision that shaded my home with trees and provided bushes as good places for hide and seek. Whoever saw that old picture for the first time didn't see lack. They saw promise.

Back in the 1990s we sold our little farm outside of Nashville in Robertson County, Tennessee. It was a tough decision made easier by the enthusiasm of the buyers. There was some shade in the front but the first task they tackled was to plant trees along the sunny side of the house. She reminded me of the old saying, "Those who are wise plant trees even though they may not live long enough to enjoy the shade."

That makes me wonder. What seeds am I planting? What do I want my harvest to reflect?

The natural world is teeming with seeds. Sometimes the planting is intentional like the new trees that will one day shade the farmhouse. Sometimes the planting is accidental like the dandelions sprinkled across our lawn. Each can yield results.

There are seeds of trees and flowers but as I learned from life experience, other things can be planted and yield results. If fact, there are significant things we plant daily through our thoughts, words and deeds.

Thoughts are powerful. Is your glass half-empty or half-full? This classic question still rings true. Studies show that we look for things throughout the day that affirm what we already believe. It's called confirmation bias. Just like to a hammer everything is a nail, the filter you view the day with can directly affect you and those you interact with. What thoughts will you be remembered for?

Words are powerful. The harsh ones are often the words that stick with us the longest. As I worked in critical care, too many times did I witness old family wounds slashed open by harsh and thoughtless words. Things said in moments of stress and tragedy. What if my words became seeds of kindness or hope? The first step would be to become aware of what I am going to say before I say it.

Deeds are powerful. Especially those actions we do without thinking. They really reflect who we are at our core. Anybody can hold it together and act right for a while but what happens when fatigue or frustration sets in, or nobody is watching? That's the challenge. Those deeds are the true reflection of who you are, not the happy façade so many of us work so hard to maintain.

Thoughts, words and deeds affect everyday life. They are also the means to build the future. One day you will be the nameless ancestor. The decisions you make today affect the future for you as well as those who will one day carry your DNA. The choices you make now can have a positive effect.

- Thoughts: Set your intention for the day and decide that you will be a force for good in any way possible.
- Words: Think about what you are going to say. If your words were bullets, would you be spraying them about so carelessly?
- Deeds: Actions speak louder than words. An open heart taps

into your compassion so that you may resonate with those who need lifting up.

The story is yours. Now what are you going to make of it?

Rebuilding After COVID

"It's relentless. What am I supposed to do with all of this emotion?" The heartsick words of the young doctor jumped out at me from the podcast. The interviewer's voice was calm. The doctor's voice strained with emotion as he prepared to make another COVID19 death notification call to a family dreading the news they were about to hear. Another death. Another family. This wasn't the kind of work he signed on for.

You are awash in a tsunami of Coronavirus. If you aren't on the front lines, then you are on the next tier knowing full well you could easily be swept into the chaos that's developed in what seems like no time at all. It's not IF, you and your family will be touched by this virus, but WHEN. And as a nurse, a first responder, there's a good chance it will touch your life in one way or another.

But you are not a victim, you are a casualty of an international assault on life as we know it. As difficult as this moment of history might be, remember this isn't just about you. Just like the virus attacks the body, it is attacking our health care system. An essential part of that is the assault on the collective life, the esprit de corps, that incredible teamwork, of health care.

Self-isolation is not a luxury for health care workers who are daily facing the fight against the COVID19 Coronavirus. Suiting up to do mortal combat with an invisible enemy is tough any day. But these patients are different. They could be you. They could be me. They could be your grandma scared to die alone. But you will be there caring for them and giving them everything you have because this work is not just what you do, it's who you are.

This is special work you've been called to so let's get to it. So let's get you through this.

> "How very little can be done under the spirit of fear."-
>
> Florence Nightingale

Let's take a two-fold approach to this.

First, the immediate question. How are you going to get through today?

- *Step one*: Stop for just a moment. Take a deep breath and step away. Become aware of who you are and where you are. Change your energy if only for a moment. If you can do it physically, like go to the break room or to the bathroom, then take just a minute. If that's not an option, then step to the side. Stop the momentum and breathe.

- *Step two*: Catch yourself. Become aware. Focus on right here right now. When you react to situations around you it is the authentic you responding or is it your exhausted autopilot who is running the show?

- *Step three*: Consider your resources. You are a winner at surviving. You are smart, intuitive and aware. Those qualities are an extra shield of protection. Clarify what you want or need and be open to what resources come your way.

- *Step four*: Stay nimble. Creative solutions have already appeared and there are more on the way. As a front-line worker during this crisis you know the problems better than anyone. You also see solutions. Stay open to possibilities.

- *Step five*: Be confident of both your strengths and your limitations. Our strengths lead us through the toughest times but remember this. The heroes in the comic books are two dimensional drawings and even Superman had his kryptonite over which he had no power. Do the best with what you have but don't beat yourself up. You are doing the best you can

Second, and when you are ready, let me help you.

There is a formula that predicts recovery following a major disaster. The length of the initial stage suggests how long recovery will take. Full recovery takes time. Sometimes recovery takes years.

What you are experiencing on the frontlines of the COVID19 crisis is unprecedented. There is little time or place to maintain your professional space. You are pushed to your limits in a space that is anchored in fear and unknowing.

There's a name for what you as a health care worker are experiencing.

"Second Victim" refers to the personal and professional impact on health care workers following a patient safety incident. Initially this work focused on physicians but further study shows that any clinician can be adversely affected by these events.

This is what you are facing on the frontlines of the COVID19 battle. And is normal to see only the failures as you second guess your skills and your knowledge.

But you are not a victim. You are a casualty of war and once this is behind you there is more work to do.

Once this is over, how will you respond?

- · Will you leave your profession?
- · Will you stay as a wounded healer and do what you can?
- · Or will you use this as a springboard to something new.

When you are ready let's look at where you are and what you want next.

In a study on listening that I did with critical care nurses we discovered that deep listening can lead to deep connection. Deep connection can lead to transformation. Together let's try a different way to respond to the new health care world. Let me show you a new way as we listen with ears, eyes, attention and hear.

Bolero

Maurice Ravel's song, "Bolero" is a popular classical music composition whose slow, deliberate beat might show up in the elevator music or as background music in a movie. It begins with the steady tap...tap...tap of the snare drum. Throughout the whole piece the beat never wavers.

My local community orchestra recently included "Bolero" in its fall music program. The drum is only one of several solos including the flute and piccolo. There's also the clarinetist whose full tones spilled out from the stage to wrap us in a cozy cloak of sound.

The ending brings relief from the dramatic tension methodically built by the orchestra. What began so simply builds to a tremendous wall of sound created by the full force of the orchestra. Throughout it all, guiding the pace and the intensity is a single drum tapping the rhythm and moving the music steadily forward.

The Drummer

Two years ago, the drummer played with another orchestra that had "Bolero" on their program. They were counting on her to do as she had in this performance which was to anchor the whole orchestra with a very difficult part of the music.

For months she diligently practiced her part over and over again as she gained the physical stamina to maintain that steady pace for over fifteen minutes, the full length of the piece. Then she had to maintain control as she led the gradual crescendo that led to a spectacular ending. Tap…tap…tap.

But the plan went awry. At the last moment the other orchestra pulled out on her. After months of concentrated work, she was told, "I don't exactly know how to say this but we're going in a different direction. We won't be able to use you."

These heavy words fell hard on the musician and while they can be heavy at any time, these carried an extra burden. All that work went down the drain. Or so she thought.

A Change of Pace

There is a saying that there are three answers to prayer: "yes," "no," and "not now." Sometimes what we get is better than what we wanted.

The drummer's work was not for nothing. Her opportunity came and she was ready. She played a spectacular solo that set the pace for the whole orchestra and drew us all into her beautiful performance.

After the performance, the director acknowledged each solo player, but he held the drummer's introduction until last. He told the audience that the drum was integral to the success of this song, and it was nothing without a good percussionist.

How much harder that performance would have been for the whole orchestra if this single person, the drummer, wasn't in control of her craft. She was skilled. She knew this music. She was ready.

The drummer's story dovetailed with a recent conversation I had with Ralph Skiano, principal clarinetist with the Detroit Symphony. His book *Behind the Screen*, succinctly maps the preparation required for a professional music audition – the showpiece of a musician's skills and its preparation must be absolutely intentional.

Skiano's focus is music but as I read his book, I realized that his crucial steps for preparation have a much broader application especially for anyone who wants to achieve a dream.

Decide on Your Goal

The first step of preparation is the decision to do "it," whatever your dream or your goal might be. Perhaps you never finished school because you stopped just a few hours short of your degree.

My friend Larry had a dream. He wanted to attend seminary, but he didn't have the required college degree. Through a remarkable series of events, not only was he accepted back into the program he had left years earlier, but the same professor was still teaching. He did not have to start from scratch. Larry had the dream and the dream embraced him, found a way to make it happen. He completed seminary and became a very effective minister.

If finishing school is a dream, even if it begins with earning your GED, it is possible to create a fuller life. A GED can open a lot of doors including getting an associates degree or a specialized certification at a community college.

What if reaching that dream not only makes you eligible for a better job but your employer might offer tuition assistance? Does that seem impossible? It's not if that is your dream. Don't discount yourself. There's help. Don't talk yourself out of a better future.

Commit

After you set your goal, the next step is to commit to it. Commitment is an internal action. It's the way to get the ball rolling.

There is a page from an old calendar that I have kept taped to my desk lamp for over thirteen years. "There is magic in setting goals. It sets into motion a powerful psychological, spiritual, and emotional force. Things begin to happen."-Anonymous.

Practice

The next step is to practice the skills you need to achieve your dream. A musician spends an incredible number of hours playing the audition music over and over again until it is as easy as breathing. That repetition works the skill into your muscle memory and then into your soul.

Practice can shift the knowledge you carry from your head to your heart. When that happens, you own it. It is yours and it comes with your unique take on whatever it is you are trying to achieve.

As many involved in sports know, the process of practice also crafts your character as you push yourself to discover your limits. Whether it is practicing at the swimming pool at 5:00 AM every morning or pushing yourself to run one more lap, the process shapes who you become.

I heard of a man who many years ago missed earning a place on the Olympic track team by just seconds. He said, "I may not have made the team, but I am an Olympian. I trained on the Olympic level. I never made it to the big time, but the process put me in the big game."

It is the same whether you do shift work and know the ins and outs of your machine better than anyone else or if your computer skills guide you without thinking. Whatever your dream, keep honing your skills. They may be the key to open your next door.

And Finally, Perform

The ultimate step is performance. Performance is the sum of skill, talent, and hard work. They come together to show just how good you are at what you do. It is a time to present your mastery of the task and who you have become in the process.

For the auditioning musician, it is the moment when they stand alone on stage for their audition, proving they can perform to the orchestra's standard. For others, it might be an opportunity that comes where you can showcase your skills in your work or a time where you can step out from the crowd and sing your song.

Dreams can change but it doesn't mean they are lost. Ask the drummer. She well knows the dream might just show up in ways you would never expect.

Be ready.

PART VII

It Takes a Village
COMMUNITY

Mirror Talk

I SUSPECT I am not the only child in the world who closed herself in the bathroom to practice her acceptance speech. Mine was for the 'Best Actress' Academy Award. I embraced my future as the world's greatest actress when I was in the second grade. Of course, the first step was to begin practicing my acceptance speech.

As I stood and tilted my head to present the best version of myself, the most appropriate words seamlessly streamed from my mouth. "I would like to thank my mother, my father, my sister...." You get the idea. I was brilliant.

These harmless practices are pantomime. Marcel Marceau and other talented mimes convey the outward motions of communication without speech. As brilliant as they are, what they do stands independent of true interaction. They are in complete control, and what is missing, is another person.

It's like hitting a tennis ball against the garage door. The game is static. You are in control of the speed and direction of the ball as it returns to you. Ultimately, you are in control because you're the only player.

It's a different game entirely if you are on the tennis court with someone else. That static solo game has become a dynamic interchange between two people. Now, since there is no way to anticipate the direction or speed of the ball, both participants are challenged to fully engage.

Perhaps it comes from living alone through the lockdown, but I am finding that as the world slowly blossoms open, I must relearn some of my social skills like conversation.

During the lockdown I was in control of my environment. Except for zoom meetings or brief phone calls I could go for days without speaking to anyone. I didn't have to dress nicely except from the waist up and as long as the mess didn't show up on the video feed, I didn't even have to do much housework.

In other words, I was hitting a ball against the wall, and as hard as my cat tried, she never mastered the art of conversation.

We are social animals. So, it feels good to be back to interacting in person. Facial gestures, body language, and tone of voice don't always translate electronically. Yet those nuances enrich our interactions, particularly in conversation. It is good for our souls to reconnect with friends and family and see them face to face.

However, in the time of isolation, it appears some of us forgot basic conversational skills. Public discourse acquired a razor-sharp edge with no space to interact on any level other than that of standing in front of the bathroom speaking to oneself. Sometimes it feels as if instead hitting the conversational ball back and forth there are two parallel solo games going on with little or no common ground.

How this happened I do not know. What I do know is that it doesn't have to be this way.

We have the power to choose our reactions. In so doing, it's important to remember that kindness counts. Politeness is necessary. These ideals are essential to maintain because without them conversation shuts down and without conversation, there is no way to connect.

Clare Biedenharn, DMin, BCC

In the listening study discussed in my book *Heart to Heart: Spiritual Care through Deep Listening*, the outcome was rather remarkable. We discovered that deep listening leads to deep connection. Deep connection leads to transformation.

Finding the connection with another establishes a common spot in which to meet and that's what is sorely needed at this time.

Of course, this problem of poor communication is as old as humankind. The pandemic didn't help that. But as we move out of our isolation toward common ground, there are questions given to us by Socrates that can guide us back to civil discourse.

"Is it true? Is it necessary? Is it kind?"

Once words are spoken, they cannot be taken back.

So, give yourself a moment to pause and reflect before you respond. To paraphrase from the Bible, "Speak to others as you would have them speak to you."

Secret Code

THERE I WAS. One of the class regulars standing chest deep in the brisk water as our swimming fitness instructor put us through our paces. A small group of us with ages ranging from 42 to 95 years old gather throughout the week at 7:00 am. As a group we have grown close, and we know that the class meets unless the public schools close. That's the signal that the roads are too bad to travel, so class is cancelled.

On this morning, someone new joined us. We all smiled and introduced ourselves and as the exercise began it was obvious that she knew her way around a swimming exercise class. She slid easily into the basic routine but then came the "Kate Kick."

The "Kate Kick" is named for a previous instructor that loved that particular exercise.

The regulars automatically began the familiar kicking pattern. However, all the action is under water, so it's not obvious what we're doing unless you already know. Out of the corner of my eye I saw our new person trying to figure out what we were doing. She didn't know what the "Kate Kick" was. She didn't know the secret code.

From a socially safe distance I directed her on the Kate Kick pattern. It consists of a front to back straight leg kick, and then a side kick, then pattern repeats. Immediately she caught on and the class proceeded.

A few exercises later the instructor called for the "BC Circle." The new person looked at me and I told her that it was moving your leg in a big circle in one direction and then reverse.

The "BC circle" is named for our 95-year-old participant. That's his favorite exercise.

As we left the pool it struck me that what just happened in class occurs consistently in daily life. We assume that others know what we're talking about and that defines the way we do things. We say hello, judge the person to be like us and then proceed with the language we are comfortable with. We assume they know what we know and see the world the way we do.

If they don't, then we assume there's a problem with them, not a problem in communication.

I once attended a meeting about enriching Sunday School practices in rural churches. The presenter needed a few volunteers to help with a demonstration. I was feeling brave and volunteered. He asked us to come to the front and just say hello and greet each other. That wasn't hard at all.

We waited for instructions for the demonstration to begin when he said, "That feels pretty good, doesn't it? You know each other and it's good to be together today. But if you aren't a member of this group, what do you see?"

Surprised, we looked around and realized that while we were smiling and saying hello to each other, we naturally formed a circle. Our faces were turned toward each other so we formed a closed group. What the rest of the world saw was only our backs.

We were part of a friendly group, but we didn't realize that our familiarity and our comfort with each other was creating a barrier to those outside the group.

How much exclusion comes without thinking? Our words, our body language, or our intentions can say a lot about us without our knowing. Without even realizing it we are conveying a message.

So you might consider this. What is your secret code? Do you have your own version of the "Kate Kick" and the "BC Circle?" What are your assumptions and how might they shape how you communicate with others?

Being Number One

"ONE, TWO, THREE." My 4-year-old grandson carefully counted and pointed to each of us sitting side by side on the sofa. Of course, he counted himself as one. His father, my son, sat in the middle and was assigned the number two spot. I, on the far end, was given the number three.

He solemnly counted another time as he pointed to us. "One, two, three."

I said, "Well aren't you smart!" Then I gave him a mischievous grin and said, "But remember. *I* am always Number One."

That caught him by surprise. My grandson was speechless at this turn of events. His jaw dropped and his eyes grew big as his little brain tried to figure out what just happened. "No!" he said as he patted his chest. "*I'm* Number One."

Then my son grinned and said, "No wait. *I'm* Number One. You know. It's all in your perspective!"

Then my grandson read the mischief in our faces, and he played along with us. With a grandiose gesture like a politician speaking on the nightly news he said, "No. Don't forget. I'm Number One," and together we shared a good laugh.

I smiled and remembered our time together as I drove the interstate highway toward home.

Suddenly a flock of geese so big that it seemed to fill the sky blasted into my vision. It was late afternoon, and the winter sun threw long shadows over the road. The geese appeared from out of nowhere and they startled me much like my playfulness had my grandson the day before. Once my brain figured out what happened, I watched the birds make their focused way across the sky.

I grew up in the city and never thought much about geese. Until that time, I only saw them as big noisy birds that pooped a lot in parking lots and honked at each other as they flew across the sky. Then years ago, I read an article that showed me another side.

- Why do they fly in a 'V' formation? Flying that way saves energy and helps them fly much farther as each goose uses the updraft of the wings immediately ahead of them. Much as a plane needs wind to lift it up to take-off, the air created by the bird ahead of it makes the flight much less strenuous.
- Geese stay close to each other to follow this path of least resistance, and their honking is a way to communicate in flight.
- If a goose gets sick, one or two other birds land and stay with it until it either heals or dies.
- Geese mate for life and if the partner dies, the remaining one finds another so that they don't have to live alone.

The lead bird has the hardest job. It is the one that hits the solid wall of air and sets up the chain of updrafts for those behind it. The following birds have the benefit of the updraft from the bird immediately before it. The leader begins the process.

As I watched, I noticed the front bird, the one blazing the trail through the undisturbed sky, dropped back in line with the birds that it was just leading. The leader had done its part. It was time to rest and cruise in the updraft along with the others.

Then the miracle happened. Without missing a beat, as the lead bird dropped back, another goose seamlessly moved ahead to take its place. There was a new leader and when that bird tires it too will drop back, and another will take its place. This natural rhythm propels the flock forward and gets it where it needs to go.

The front goose holds an essential role in the flock but as difficult as it may be, there are others who are prepared to take their turn and share the burden. They are ready to step in and take their turn as Number One. They know their task and they are ready.

Geese have something to teach us. Much like them, each of us can stand (or fly) individually. However, when we combine our talents together, they become much stronger than those that stand alone. Together, we bring a much broader set of gifts to offer the world. Together, we fly farther.

The sofa held three generations. My grandson, my son and I sat side by side. Each of us could claim to be Number One. Each of us brings a talent. I bring a life full of experience.

My son is practical and always planning. And my four-year-old grandson? He brings imagination, a fresh perspective, and an open heart.

We have individual gifts but when we bring them together something special can happen as they synergize and become something greater. The sum of our efforts is much greater than when we work alone. Working together, like the geese flying in the 'V' formation, we each can help our flock move forward.

Yes, we can go it alone, but the ride is a lot easier when we travel together.

Special Love

As strange as this may sound, every weekday morning I wake at 6:00 am, have a cup of coffee, say my prayers, and put on a bathing suit. At 7:30 I am at the swimming pool.

A promise brings me to the pool each morning. After my husband died, my son mentioned that his dad's main concern was that I'd become a hermit.

It is a comfortable place to come. There's a rhythm to entering, saying hello to the greeter, and checking in with my well-worn tag on my key chain. Then I join the class that is filled with familiar faces, and we laugh and share our daily lives with each other in a loose but committed community.

The other day something happened that bothered me.

The parking lot is one of those typical seas of blacktop divided in the middle by a narrow sidewalk. Parking is straightforward. The standard operating procedure is to drive into the parking lot and if there are no empty spaces on one side then, follow the arrows, park on the other side facing the first side of cars. The cars are parked nose to nose

This particular morning, I had just pulled into my spot when in the space right beside my door a truck startled me as it roared into and then through the parking space and kept on going.

At first, I thought it was out of control. The truck sped through the space, jumped the small sidewalk curb, and parked on the opposite side with its nose pointed out for a quick takeoff.

Just as I was ready to jump out and see if the driver was all right, he casually got out of the truck, grabbed his stuff, and went on into the Y.

He didn't even glance my way.

It took me a moment to collect myself as I processed what had just happened. I was stunned. Then I was angry because I was startled. Then I felt frustrated with myself for letting my day start with irritation over something so seemingly petty. Yet on some level his actions were unsettling.

Maybe my reaction was strong because, to be honest, driving over that slight sidewalk has crossed my mind. If the space opposite mine was empty, it would be extremely easy to just ease on over that little curb and keep going instead of backing up to drive all the way around.

This sounds so picky. What am I concerned about? I wasn't harmed and for now neither was the curb.

But what if I hadn't stopped to unplug my phone and simply opened the door when I parked? What if the driver in his rush hadn't seen a person on that sidewalk?

The biggest question though is what happens if we all break the sometimes inconvenient but tacitly agreed upon rules that shape our lives?

Some are embedded in our laws. Drive on the correct side of the road to dramatically reduce the chance of a head-on collision. Others are more subtle. Cover your mouth when you cough.

There's an underlying fear that our world is falling apart. Reporters make a good living reinforcing that idea. The media often has us searching for something or someone outside of ourselves for the problem. It presents an unwritten message that if we could only find the source of the problem our lives would fall back into place and the world will be restored.

- Where is our own place in this scenario?
- In what way do we contribute?
- Do we add to the chaos, or do we choose to hold in in check?
- Do we park in the correct parking space, or do we jump the curb?

We do have a say in all of this.

We are in a symbiotic relationship of change as we and our institutions dance to accommodate whatever challenge comes next. The systems that worked in the past for us are evolving. But I have to admit I sometimes miss the comfort of a reliable world.

It is important to remember, though, that as overwhelming as life may be, we are not without power. I have a choice in how I react and my contribution to the solution is small but consistent.

I feel safe when I follow the unspoken rules that bind us all together. I drive on the correct side of the road. I yield to pedestrians at crosswalks, and I allow space for a bike rider.

I do it not just because it is socially correct but because I have respect for those who might be affected by my poor choice. I feel better because these small decisions stack up one by one and reflect who I am as a person.

These little acts may appear to be no big deal, but each time we decide on order over disorder something else is happening too. We are expressing love.

In the late 1990s, I attended a meeting at a small retreat center in the remote, piney Mississippi woods. It lasted two or three days and I must admit that I don't remember the topic of the meeting. What does stand out for me is the spirit of the presenter.

The leader shared with us that one of his real pleasures, especially when he's leading a retreat, is take time for a long, hot shower before he begins his day. It sets his mood and helps him gather his thoughts before he steps in front of an audience.

That morning, however, just as he settled in under that spray of hot water, he realized something. The retreat center was small. What if his long shower took all the hot water and there was none for anyone else?

With that thought he quickly finished his shower so there would be enough for anyone who might enjoy a hot shower too.

He wasn't telling the story to draw attention to himself but to show how the expression of love comes in many ways.

Love has many voices. Sometimes it comes as romance or through family or deep friendships. That strong feeling that resonates in the heart expresses itself as many facets of love.

The love the retreat leader expressed that day was what the Greeks called agape or universal love. The kind of love encompasses all things, not just individuals.

It's the kind of love that comes without condition because it simply exists. That's the kind of love that comes through empathy for another especially when you've 'walked a mile in their shoes.'

It's also called God's love.

We're all in the same boat as the changes swirl around us and we hold on for the ride. Our power lies in how we choose to react.

I admit it. I've been tempted to jump the curb too. But by following the rules, spoken and unspoken, I entered into an agreement with society. That implicit agreement is that I, by following accepted ways of doing things, am making a covenant between me and those around me. I'm saying that what I do can affect others just as their actions can affect me.

That is not to say that the rules of society are flawless. Many have suffered because of misinterpretation of the rules or, even worse, selected application. These rules, however, have shown over time that order in society makes things a little bit nicer. If we know the expectations and follow through with our actions, then daily living is just a bit better.

For the man in the truck, this is no big deal. His tires are big and strong. He's not worried about it. He probably didn't even give it another thought. The concrete path is narrow. But how does that truck weight affect that slip of concrete over time?

Even more significantly, what if there had been a person who believed they were safe on that little slab of concrete? What if in his rush he hadn't seen that person until it was too late?

It startled me and frightened me too. Unexpectedly, the rhythm of my morning changed.

We've all grown up with a pretty good idea of what is or isn't acceptable within our culture. In a way, that's the minimum expectation of behavior. But each of us has the capacity to do and be more. That is a standard we set for ourselves.

In a healthcare setting, a nurse works within the standards of care set by their healthcare community. That includes those set out by the licensure board and as well as the facility for which they work.

After watching nurses in action for decades, I feel comfortable saying that there is another standard of care that nurses set that goes beyond just 'following the rules.'

There is a line of care that they will consistently provide. If they are unable to do that, moral distress, or even moral injury, results because the inability to provide it is an assault on their personal core values.

It is the same for each of us. Personal core values create our North Star, a point of reference as we navigate through life.

These values provide the personal standard of behavior that that reflects our core beliefs about ourselves and our place in society. They sit nestled within society expectations, but it's a personal choice that affects how I feel about myself.

As I sit in the parking space I am faced with a choice. I can take the high road and follow the parking lot's accepted standard of behavior or not. Or I can jump the curb because it's expedient with no thought of broken bodies or broken curbs.

Each day we are faced with big and little decisions. "Do you want cream in that coffee?" "Am I going to slip through the intersection on the yellow caution light or will I sit through that terribly long red light?"

Some are significant. Most are not.

If we consistently make decisions based on our better nature, we are all better off as we choose a good path or vibe for our lives.

Airport Realizations
FLYING

Not long ago I was faced with a conundrum. I signed a contract to appear at a national nurse's conference in Orlando. I signed it before another opportunity to work with nurses appeared. No matter how I maneuvered my schedule, I was stuck with flying to get back to work with my new clients.

Oh, and I should tell you I don't like to fly.

To feel completely at the mercy of companies and security and other things that are beyond my control makes me anxious. I take responsibility for my own messes (like falling asleep and missing the plane to Rome), but I don't like theirs.

If I hadn't signed a contract to appear at the conference, I could have talked myself out of the trip. In the end, there was no way around it—I had to fly. Despite my efforts to avoid the drama du jour on the daily news, it seemed that a current pain point is the connection between planes.

I thought I was being smart when I booked a very early direct flight. Sure, the time was inconvenient, but when I had to call on the parking lot angels to help me find one of the last available spots, I once again questioned my travel decision.

The escalator landed me in the middle of a security line that snaked its way across the lobby, appearing and disappearing around nooks and crannies.

I was lucky. My TSA pass got me to a short line where the agent said, "I just heard that other line just topped 1,000 people."

What happened? What happened to that age of transportation that seemed to work so seamlessly? That era was different in so many ways.

I was seven years old on my first flight but that was a different world. For that glamourous trip I wore my starched pink Easter dress with a hat and gloves and my little suitcase was free checked baggage. Now, I was sporting a heavily layered look so that my clothes, brochures and give away pens could all be squeezed into a backpack that could be jammed under the seat. Back then, I got a hot meal on glass dishes. Now, I provided my own package of cheese crackers. I'm still trying to figure out where in a seat space the size of a can of tuna my legs were supposed to go.

Returning Home

The conference went well. I did my presentation for the nurses, and, with dread, I turned my eyes to the trip back home. The trip here was relatively bland, but so many questions came and stirred my anxiety. If the security line was so long on the trip down, what would it be like here? When should I text an Uber? The sky was looking ominous. What would that mean for the flight?

One by one, answers arrived as the trip stretched out before me to become a long day of travel. The first text of many that would march across my phone screen that day came on the way to the airport. "Delay in departure."

Those gray clouds brought rain and heavy lightning. Basic maintenance required for takeoff was impossible. Planes arrived but were unable to leave and created a bottleneck that took hours to clear.

The one-hour delay became two, three, four, five, and six hours. As the clock progressed, the waiting area grew thick with passengers. Our eyes scanned the departure screens. Our ears strained to hear muffled announcements from airport staff.

It became obvious to me that *we no longer live in a hat and glove world.*

The little girls in princess dresses and happy families that met me when I first arrived in Orlando were replaced by an eclectic group marching by. What I saw when I arrived was Fantasyland; where I was now was 'Realityland.'

This parade of weary travelers wearing all kinds of different clothes and carrying a variety of bags and snacks reflects the 'new' travel. They bring with them many colors and nationalities. When I was a child, only people who looked like me took glamourous plane rides. Now travel opens us to the world.

Together these hundreds of people and I shared a desire to be safely at home in our beds, but we shared something else as well.

When we finally prepared to board the plane, I looked around at my fellow travelers and I realized something remarkable. Even though we were jammed into a relatively small space in a very unpleasant situation:

- The crowd stayed relatively calm, and there were no temper flares.
- Strangers chatted and as the evening progressed a camaraderie based on shared experience emerged.
- The babies weren't crying.

Travel these days is different. The seven-year-old girl I was may have enjoyed the momentary glamour but the woman I've become doesn't

AIRPORT REALIZATIONS

need its trappings. What is important is not the baggage I carry but how I handle it.

The anxieties that once shaped me now were comforted by:

- The kind strangers who assured me that they would wake me up if I fell asleep while waiting.
- The courtesy we showed each other as strangers as we waited in the long line at the ladies' bathroom.
- The kindness of the fellow passenger who shared her supper with me.

Courtesy and respect haven't disappeared like white gloves and hats. Nobody wanted to be delayed on their journeys home, but we stayed calm and made the best of it.

I'm kind of proud of us for that.

PART VIII

Going Forward Despite Myself
GROWTH

Liminal Space

A CONCEPT FROM MY BOOK *Heart to Heart*, CAME TO MIND AS I WATCHED A STRUGGLING PATIENT CLIMB OUT OF THEIR CAR AND PUSH THROUGH THE FRONT DOOR OF THE PHYSICAL THERAPIST'S OFFICE. AS MY EYES FOLLOWED THEIR ACTIONS, I GARNERED MY OWN STRENGTH AND MOVED FROM MY CAR TO THE VERY SAME OFFICE.

How did I end up here? In my haste to fill the bird feeders before the Christmas ice storm arrived, I slipped on my back porch steps. Before I knew it, I found myself on the ground at the bottom step covered in birdseed with my knee twisted at a very odd angle.

The emergency department's x-ray reported that my knee was not broken. However, the big brace wrapped around my leg spoke to me and said, "Sit back. This might take a while."

The brace was correct. Through an unfortunate slip, I moved from the world of wellness to that of being a patient. I even had my very own name band wrapped around my wrist. To work my way back to wellness took time. There was my own stubbornness to face. Most of the work happened in that in between space of time and transition called *liminal*.

The liminal is like a threshold: the small piece of wood at the bottom of the door frame that forms the slim space between two rooms. This space is unique in that it is not quite *here* and not quite *there* yet holds a bit of both and provides a transition between the two.

Watching my fellow patient hobble from car to office door reminded me of the 2016 study by Pigott, Hargreaves, and Power cited in my book, *Heart to Heart*. The study explored the use of holding spaces in commercial buildings. These are spaces in which an individual may pause and reorient before moving on to the next space in their journey.

Transitional Space

Many churches have a space in the back by the entry doors where one can pause before entering the sanctuary. Medical offices have a room for those waiting to see the healthcare provider. These areas not only have chairs for waiting but also provide a **transitional space** that helps one prepare to switch paradigms.

In this case, the shift was from wellness to needing care. A transitional space is the space of preparation. Only recently did I discover its importance.

My doctor's waiting room was empty when I entered, and that surprised me. I expected to share the space with others, imagining we would acknowledge each other and wait for the call to the next step of moving behind the reception counter. Instead, I was checked in and then whisked directly down the hall to the examination room without a moment to adjust to the office space. The unexpected move felt awkward and disorienting.

I guess I could have asked for a moment to catch my breath, but the moment only moved forward. So, I too chose to move forward. I wanted all to be well. History proves that those who can adapt to an evolving situation are more likely to survive such a transition.

"Healing takes time" is one of those axioms I've heard all my life. And as happens so often, I found the saying to be true. The accident happened at Christmas. Now, spring flowers push against the warming soil to grow and bloom in the sun.

The seasons slowly changed from one to another. Like the imperceptible growth of winter, my movements were slow and quiet through my recovery. I laid low, rested, and faithfully submitted to physical therapy. Now like spring, I was restless and ready to move back through this transitional period between hurt and healed.

Last month I set aside the cane. This month I completed a full set of tai chi movements without having to sit and rest.

The liminal space provided a holding place for me as I recovered. One day a thought struck me. Maybe we as a people have been in a similar place, as we move on to a world of change that continues to unfold:

- Is it possible that in the quiet, liminal space since the lockdown, we tapped into our resilience as we moved from the need for care and cure to become healed and whole?
- Is it possible that we as a people are adapting to life's changes and transitioning into something new?
- Is it possible that after this time of quiet reorientation, we are ready to emerge and embrace an ever-evolving change for the good?

These questions came to me not as I lay on the ground covered with birdseed with the idea of recovery far in the future. It was in the quiet time as I discovered my limitations were temporary and that healing could occur.

The questions came as I moved back through the threshold of transition to embrace a life where wholeness and health were possible. Little acts of determination moved me slowly but surely back to a healthy life.

We are not chained to a negative past, and we don't have to carry the negative forward with us. It might take a little time and require a little stubbornness but the possibility for wholeness remains.

Take time to acknowledge what you've survived and continue forward through it, and don't rush the process. Growth awaits ahead. It comes through the quiet times of reflection.

The Holly Tree

My neighbor and I stood in her driveway in the deep summer heat. She lives next door and has lived in the neighborhood longer than most. This was the first time she and I talked since my husband's funeral a few months before. She kindly gave me her condolences and I accepted them. It was good to think of him again.

We both squinted from the glare as she turned her eyes to the back of my yard. My eyes followed hers as she said, "I was worried about my favorite tree. I love that holly tree. I was afraid we were going to lose it there for a while."

She grew up on a farm in the country and her authoritative voice resonated with my deepest fear. I think she was right. I think I came close. The thought of losing anything else was very sobering.

I almost killed the holly tree. That tree is in *my* yard, and it is *my* responsibility, and I almost killed it.

She said she was afraid we were going to cut it down as part of our big renovation. Mother rented the house to two young men who did not treat the property kindly. This refuge required a major overhaul before we could move in.

THE HOLLY TREE

A lot changed but I could never harm that holly tree. It was too beautiful and besides, my mother loved it too. To lose the tree would be like losing her and my husband all over again.

Since my mother died, I've been living in her old house. She bought it after my daddy died. The larger, grander house I grew up in, the one that seemed too small for two parents and four children, became too big for a solitary set of footprints.

When she bought this little house, my sister lived around the corner. The location was a good fit for them both. Then, my sister moved away, and my mother moved closer to my nephew. She kept the house and rented it because nobody else really wanted it.

Mother dangled this house as an incentive for us to move home as James' health declined. We needed help and home was the place to come. Our house in New Orleans had not yet sold. So, we at least had a place to stay while James walked his slow steps toward death.

To me, it isn't just a house. My mother lived here. My husband died here. My sons were school-aged children when they chased each other around that old holly tree. I have deep feelings about this house and its care is up to me.

And that includes the holly tree.

It isn't just some bush. The house was built in 1920, and the tree might have been proudly planted by those who built it. Holly trees grow slowly. So, it has been around awhile. It is now taller than my home. A tree like that deserves respect and care.

Like I said, the house needed work to be livable. An alley runs along the back and as part of our big renovation project we extended the little gravel patch my mother used for parking to a semi-circle that crossed the backyard. It wasn't too close to the tree roots or at least that's what I thought.

We clipped the bottom branches to provide space to park our cars and lined the edges of the driveway with timbers. It looked neat and clean until the yellow leaves dropped from the trees and blanketed the yard.

About six months after the completed project, I stood at the backdoor sipping a mug of coffee. Suddenly it struck me that there were a lot of yellow leaves on that evergreen tree. As I looked closer, it appeared that yellow leaves blanketed the driveway too. I got a sinking feeling.

I killed the holly tree.

That's what sunk into the pit of my stomach as I glanced out the back door and noticed that the tree didn't look very happy. It seemed like there were as many yellow leaves in the tree as there were on the ground.

I felt scared and stupid and thoughtless. Grief and shame washed over me. *What in the world was I thinking?* No driveway was more important than that beautiful tree. It splashed green in the coldest, grayest of winter days and its red berries fed the birds.

My mind scrambled to make some sense of what I saw. All I wanted was to fix it. I sprang into action. Surely there was something I could do. Surely there was some action I could take to reverse the damage that was falling from its very branches.

I soon discovered that even though the holly is an evergreen tree, that doesn't mean it doesn't lose some leaves. To grow it needs to shed. Maybe the tree was in shock. Perhaps there was still hope.

I slowed myself down and thought about the history of the tree and its resiliency. Even if this loss was more than its usual amount of leaves, the tree has already survived a lot.

I thought about its strength and what all that tree has witnessed. Was it there for the 1937 flood that inundated this whole part of town? What about the big tornado of 1975? It certainly survived that along with an untold number of assaults from the elements: rain, wind, snow, ice. This tree has seen a lot.

THE HOLLY TREE

Despite all of that, the tree is still here.

I thought, *I'm just going to give it some time.*

I watered it and fed it and gave it an encouraging word every time I drove under it to park my car. The following year when the yellow leaves dropped again, it seemed there weren't quite as many on the ground as the year before and those on the tree blended better into the remaining green leaves.

Then I realized that I needed to do the same for myself. The tree reminded me that to survive a shock, living things need a little time. They need water, food, rest, and a kind word now and then. With some support there's a good chance they will survive the shock just as my tree has and as I have too.

My shock was the loss of my husband of 41 years. For others it might be the loss of a job or any number of things the pandemic threw their way. It's been a tough stretch for most of us.

Yet it's important to not gloss over loss. The things of the past need to be grieved so that the hurt and memories don't lock us into expectations for a life that isn't ever going to be the same.

Acknowledge the pain and release it. Otherwise, it will remain a heavy weight like an anchor dragging behind a speedboat. You can keep moving forward but it's a lot easier without that extra load.

Like the tree, to grow we need to shed.

Would I want my husband here now? A part of me says "yes!" But the part of me that saw him struggle says, "no.' Thank God he didn't have to suffer not only physically but also in other ways as we have watched our world change.

We can't control the changes around us, but we can choose how we accept them. In that choice lies our ultimate freedom.

My choice is to be as kind and accepting of myself as I was to the tree as it suffered. It has taken me a while to reach this point. I realized that to turn my eyes forward to the future and away from an inalterable past wasn't being disloyal to him. My acceptance honors what we had and who we were together. It provides a strong foundation for whatever lies ahead.

It's taken a while, but now I see this is a very good place to be.

Like the tree, I'll get past this rough spot.

Like the tree I will survive.

Like the tree I will thrive rooted in this space where I choose to be.

I have hope and that is good.

Pass the Baton

THE DAY WAS FINALLY HERE. Had it taken months or only weeks to gather the girls into a somewhat organized track team? Our after-school training for the one big meet against the other elementary schools seemed to stretch out for forever. Our school playground was too tight for all of us to run, jump, or pass the baton. So, we tracked the length of the longer races by counting the garbage cans as we sailed down the alley behind the school.

It was a little hard to find a place for me on the team since I was so much larger than the other kids. I had already reached my adult height of 5'7". So, I was at least a head taller than every other kid in the school including the boys. Usually, the teacher placed me in awkward spots like the back of the line so they could tell with a glance that the students were still together.

Running was something I loved and with the track team I was competing with others but also competing against myself. And, of course, having a crush on my coach/teacher was an additional motivator. I respected him and I wanted him to be proud of me.

PASS THE BATON

I tried out for different events, but the coach decided that with my long legs and steady pace that the third runner of four in the 440-relay race was a good place for me. For weeks we practiced the run including handing off the baton. The receiving runner started running and picking up speed just as the previous runner lined up to pass the baton. Once in hand the next runner kept running to pass the baton all the way around.

The day of the meet arrived. We were excited and scared. This was before Title 9 allowed equal access to sports for girls. So, being on a team with an opportunity to compete was both a little scary and a little thrilling.

The meet was at the stadium where my parents watched high school football decades earlier. Now it was my big day, and I had my mind and heart set on victory. Each of us took our places around the track and suddenly we heard the crack of the starter gun, and the race was on!

Our runner #1 took off and sped to runner #2. Then as #1 approached, #2 prepared to match her pace and she found it easy to pass the baton to #2.

I watched #2's coming toward me and in my mind began synching my steps with hers. She came close and I moved ahead reaching behind me for the baton. We made a great pass but then something happened. I thought I had a firm grip on it, but I fumbled.

I dropped the baton.

This had never happened in practice. What am I to do? I hesitated and decided to leave it. I kept running. When I reached #4, she looked confused as I slapped her hand. "Go!" I yelled and she took off. We didn't get an opportunity to pass the baton. I didn't know I was supposed to stop and pick it up.

I thought finishing the race was what was most important. I didn't realize that the baton was the critical part of the puzzle.

It wasn't until the end of the race that I discovered just how serious my error was. Without the baton, we were disqualified. All that the training was for nothing. My relay team went home empty handed.

I broke into inconsolable tears. I failed. I failed my team and my coach. In my 6th grade mind, nothing could be worse.

I just didn't know the consequences of my actions. I hung my head in shame. The weight of the world rode on my shoulders.

Fast forward more than a few decades. That pang of shame hit me in the stomach as the hard memory bubbled up from some deep place. It was at a funeral. The preacher was preaching the funeral service and the familiar words from scripture about running a good race brought it all back.

> *I have fought the good fight, I have finished the race, I have kept the faith.*
>
> Timothy 4:7, NIV

Ouch. If only I could speak so confidently of my own race.

What exactly is 'the race'?

It's not the proverbial 'rat race' of life that comes from busy, noisy lives. That competitive race of daily living makes slipping between soft sheets in bed at the end of the day feel like a moment of victory. Hallelujah! You've made it through another day.

The preacher wasn't talking about the kind of race where we're running competitively against each other in a world where the fear of scarcity motivates us to live agitated lives.

No, this other kind of race is like a stream or a current that is continually moving us forward toward a seemingly impossible prize. This prize is a life filled with love and confidence for ourselves and for others. It is a place of peace as we understand we are part of a something bigger than what we can only see and touch. There's a greater good swirling around us. We are not alone.

Each faith has a name for this place of peace. Heaven? Nirvana? Or in secular terms it could be the Self-actualization in Maslow's hierarchy of need – defined as a sense of inner peace and an understanding of your place in the universe.

Peace. What a beautiful word.

No, this race is more like the run to carry the Olympic flame around the world. There is no competition. Dedication and understanding of its significance are what keeps it moving forward. Each time a runner passes the flame to the next runner, they form another link in the chain.

It's like that for you too. You are one link in a chain forged by the generation before you. It is your heritage of light that passed to you. What you received doesn't die with you as long as you pass it on.

The baton you carry in your race is a symbol of that connection of love passed to you by your mama and daddy, grandparents, neighbors... anyone who helped shape you into the person you are today. It came to you through stories and observation of your elders. Your job is to carry it, protect it, and nourish it so you can pass it on to the next generation. That's your responsibility.

Who gave you your baton? Not everyone grew up in families who nurtured or even remembered their own spiritual heritage but from watching the world around you may have had to craft your own. It may have been passed to you by circumstances at some point, and necessity made it yours. Did hard times help you find it?

Where is your baton now? Is it still in your care or have you dropped it? Or maybe you tucked it away figuring you would pull it out if you needed it.

You need it now. We need it now.

We need the light your faith brings to the world.

Are you afraid that you're not good enough, faithful enough or whatever-else enough to complete the task given to you?

I didn't know this then, but I know it now. I could have redeemed my messed-up relay race if only I had stopped and picked up that baton. I didn't know that was permissible. I didn't know that was possible. I thought the point was just to finish. I didn't realize how important that baton was.

The good news is this. Not only is it permissible to pick that baton back up, but it is also critical that you do. The world needs your spark of light.

How is it possible to recover what you forgot you carried with you? You do it slowly and simply.

- Start by setting your intention for the day even before your first cup of coffee. Remember this is the day the Lord has made and by golly you're going to plug into it.
- Look for God in your day. Listen to how God speaks to you? Does God come to you in a big clap of thunder or in a soft whisper as you think of someone you might need to check on?
- Be grateful for those moments when you recognize God's presence. It is always there. It's just up to you to realize it.

And here's the really important part. If you have dropped your baton, pick it up, brush it off and be ready.

- When you pick it up, you state your intention to be a part of the race.
- It is something tangible, and it's your responsibility to pass it on to the next runner in the race.
- Picking it up, you honor what you have received from those who came before you

In today's world, it is more important than ever to pick it up. Have faith that someone is waiting for you to pass the baton.

It's yours to give. Pass it on.

Emerging From the Hermitage
GRANDMA TO THE RESCUE!

An almost-neon-yellow bush caught my eye.

The street was filled with trees whose buds promised spring. Blooming buttercup flowers swayed in the breeze, brushing over the daylilies with their early emergence from the ground.

The days are longer. The nights don't feel as wintry, even though I still haven't surrendered my flannel sheets!

Nature is stirring, and so am I.

This was a couple weeks ago. The nanny was out sick for a week and my son asked if I could help with my two grandsons, ages 3 and 6. Of course I said yes. My suitcase was packed and, in the car, before we got off the phone.

It was a delightful week. I live hours away from my grandchildren. Visits are usually quick weekend adventures. Thanks to us all having more time together, I had the chance to know them better as individuals, not just "the boys."

It was also a treat to have time with my son and his wife.

EMERGING FROM THE HERMITAGE

Counting Blessings

It was a good week, but before I left for home, I felt inspired to stop and count my blessings.

I got to spend time with my grandchildren. I got to spend time with my son. An absolute treasure during this busy time of his life.

To my surprise, there was another gift. Our time together gave me the opportunity to ease back into being around people.

My husband died right before I retired. Then COVID hit and the lockdown came. Social activities ceased, and the YMCA pool closed along with its daily water exercise class, my main connection with other people.

Zoom became an important link to the outside world. In the quiet of isolation my two published books emerged.

Then, even though the lockdown was over, the world seemed a little different. I was different too. I was always a bit of an extrovert, but I had grown too comfortable in my isolation.

Slowly, the world opened up again. The pool opened. Friends returned. Zoom remained an important link, but I realized that it was time to be back out around "real" people.

I thought that all I needed to do was plop myself into the middle of activity. However, the week with my grandchildren helped me realize there are steps to reintegration.

Leaving the Hermitage

First, I needed to acknowledge that there was something in my life that I outgrew. My time alone – I call it "the Hermitage" – was my refuge from the storms of life. It was here that I began healing from my husband's death. It was here that I began writing. It was here in the quiet that I reflected and pieced together the quilt of my life.

Second, I realized that this type of reflection can be sad, silly, happy, and embarrassing, but ultimately, it is good.

In the process, I forgave myself for some poor decisions and released some grudges. I realized how they drained my psyche.

Somehow, letting go of these parts that dragged me down made what remained even sweeter.

I never gave in to my grief. I survived a tough time. I was ready to get back among people.

Reintegration can be slow and easy. I learned that it's perfectly okay to listen to my body and soul, to go at an easy pace, a little bit at a time.

It will come as I'm ready and willing. I accept the changes in myself and others that come with learning to be with people again.

That week with my grandchildren was a first step. The heart of a child can lead the way if only we open ourselves and let them.

All I need now is a little more stamina and it's coming. Like building muscles, all it needs is a little exercise.

PART IX

Put It Under a Bushel? NO!
LIGHT

Good Vibrations

NOT LONG AGO I saw a sign on a clinic door that read:

"PLEASE TAKE RESPONSIBILITY FOR THE ENERGY YOU BRING INTO THIS SPACE. YOUR WORDS MATTER. YOUR BEHAVIORS MATTER. OUR PATIENTS AND OUR TEAMS MATTER. TAKE A SLOW, DEEP BREATH AND MAKE SURE YOUR ENERGY IS IN CHECK BEFORE ENTERING. THANK YOU."

That sign addressed one of life's biggest challenges: our energy. It matters and it is our responsibility to manage it.

There is an energy field extending beyond the physical body that we call our personal space. It goes with us everywhere. It's the feeling that occurs when somebody stands too close or the joy you feel when you're around someone you love. Similar to the Peanuts character "Pig Pen" who walks around in a cloud of dust, the energy you carry with you is your vibe, your dust. It's your aura. In that space, our energy interacts with others.

Last month I made a quick stop at Dollar Tree. Right inside the door, a man was pushing a cart while talking very loudly into his cellphone. He carried a chaotic presence. I avoided eye contact, said a little prayer, and dodged past him.

Just as I thought I was in the clear, he came right up behind me in the checkout line. He was still on the phone. He stood too close. He set down a lot of odd things and then, in a very loud voice, he interrupted the cashier (who was checking me out) to ask where the batteries were.

The cashier focused on ringing up my transaction. So, he asked even louder. Suddenly, in an even louder voice he confrontationally declared that he didn't have enough money for his purchases. It was like he was a black hole of energy, and he would take as much of us as we allowed. I paid and hurried out.

His energy was disruptive. My personal space told me his aura was a bit out of kilter. My first impression proved correct, so I was wise to protect my energy field when I first shielded myself with that little prayer. I had said, "I place myself in the white light of protection."

Sympathetic Resonance

Few explain the powerful effect of personal energy on others better than Dr. Jill Bolte-Taylor, a Harvard neuroanatomist. In her book, *My Stroke of Insight*, she described her experience of having a stroke from the unique perspective of being a brain scientist.

A part of her brain remained engaged with her surroundings following the stroke. As a clinical professional, she observed her post-stroke care.

One of her most profound reflections was her **awareness of the energy that each person brought into the room**. Some brought helpful, supportive energy and for them she wanted to "show up" and engage them. Then there were others, like the medical intern who handled her roughly and sucked all the energy out of the room. She called that being an energy vampire and her spirit withdrew to protect her strength.

There is science behind this feeling, and it is called **sympathetic resonance**. The term originated in music.

When playing the cello, if I place my finger in the right spot on the first string to play a 'C' note, the open fourth string named 'C' vibrates even though it is on a different string. They vibrate in sympathy with each other. They're not touching or holding hands. They just vibrate alike. One note "sets the tone" and the corresponding string follows. It works the same with any stringed instrument.

When the instrument and the air around it vibrates at the same frequency such as playing the same note, the second string vibrates *in sympathy. This phenomenon is called sympathetic resonance.*

It works for humans too. We 'resonate' and others pick up our 'vibe.'

Einstein himself stated, "It followed from the special theory of relativity that mass and energy are both but different manifestations of the same thing-a somewhat unfamiliar conception for the average mind."

You bring a vibe with you wherever you go. People around you resonate with that vibe. To that end, you have some control in how you bring your energy into the world.

How do you manage your own energy?

- *Self-awareness.* When you are aware of your own issues you are less likely to project your shortcomings onto others.
- *Keep your vibrations up.* It's up to you to care for yourself. Whatever you need to do protect or maintain your energy, do it. Keep a snack in your desk. Stop and take a few deep breaths. Meditation or quick prayer in line at the store. Music, exercise, making good choices, remaining positive. They can all help.
- *Hold your own energy no matter what.* Remember the energy vampires, the needy people who will suck the life right out of you? Hold the line on your boundaries and protect yourself. It's not personal. If they don't get your energy, they'll go on to somebody else.

- *Another Kind of Energy*. Consider for a moment the energy which is directed at you. Sometimes the energy is good and sometimes it is not. If it is not, ask angels, God or your Higher Power for protection. It is not yours if you don't accept it.
- *It's Not Always Personal*. How somebody reacts says more about them than it does about you. Some people just like to keep things stirred up. That doesn't mean you have to engage them or carry their baggage. 'No' can be a positive word.

As the sign said so well:

"PLEASE TAKE RESPONSIBILITY FOR THE ENERGY YOU BRING INTO THIS SPACE. YOUR WORDS MATTER. YOUR BEHAVIORS MATTER. OUR PATIENTS AND OUR TEAMS MATTER. TAKE A SLOW, DEEP BREATH AND MAKE SURE YOUR ENERGY IS IN CHECK BEFORE ENTERING. THANK YOU."

You always have choice in how you give and receive energy. Choose wisely.

Spokes On a Wheel

THE WINTER WIND caught my car door, but I held tight to keep it from smacking the car parked next to me. The sky was still black and the big cold front that was blowing through compounded my misery. The sign at the bank I pass each morning said 27 degrees, and that wasn't even counting the windchill factor.

I looked across the seemingly endless stretch between my car and the glowing light spilling out from the YMCA lobby door. I groaned as the age-old cartoon characters, the angel and the devil, seemed to appear on my shoulders. The little cartoon devil whispered, "Why bother? Go home and get back in that warm bed." Then the angel on the other shoulder smiled benevolently and waited for me to remember that I was here for more than exercise: I was here to see some folks.

The angel won this round. I sighed and grabbed my bag with my equipment. The icy wind was disagreeable but the light spilling out of the lobby door was like light from a lighthouse promising warmth and comfort.

In that light, I saw why I was there. My friends, my cohorts, were each funneling from scattered parked cars toward the single lobby door.

SPOKES ON A WHEEL

A Little Community

A small but faithful group of individuals gather each weekday morning at 7:30 am for water exercise class. Summer or winter we gather, although the longer, warmer days of summer make the effort much more pleasant.

For some reason we show up. My official excuse is exercise, but it is more than that. I have come to know and trust this motley group of retirees, housewives, realtors, writers, and generally remarkable individuals.

I first came because I needed to exercise and simply have a moment for myself. My husband was terminally ill. With this early class I could slip away and be home just as he woke for breakfast.

The first few times I came to the pool were hard. I didn't know anyone. I felt fat in my suit. I felt guilty about leaving my husband. Somehow, though, I pushed through my resistance. The effort was well worth it.

The exercise class welcomed me and over the years they walked with me through a lot. After James' decline and death, the widows in the class assured me that over time my broken heart would heal. The writers in the class encouraged me to start writing what became my first book. Retired teachers and military cheered me on, and from the 94-year-old who comes even more consistently than me, I learned that I have a say in my quality of life. It just takes some effort.

I love these folks. They are important to me and to my well-being.

Light by Light

As I watched everyone come to the lobby door, each brought their own light. The glow from the door seemed just a bit brighter as each stepped across the threshold to contribute to this place of warmth and welcome.

The guy who checked us in set a tone of welcoming hospitality. It was as if with each swipe of the person's entry pass, the light grew just a bit stronger.

Like the spokes of a wheel shifting energy from the wheel to the hub, our energy grows stronger as we gather and share our light with each other.

The forced lockdown of 2020 confirmed the longstanding belief that we are social animals. We need each other. Humans weren't made to be alone. We met the challenge of isolation by learning such things as Zoom etiquette or standing on a balcony to talk across a safe space to another. Or we stood outside care center windows where we could touch loved ones through glass.

A part of the isolation wasn't so bad. Home felt safe from the viruses. We could stay in our pajamas all day if we wanted, and many worked from home.

Once again, things changed and now there were new challenges. Dropping our guard to move again through the outside world was a process that was and is sometimes awkward.

We forgot that the outside world doesn't move as smoothly or as quickly as the little lockdown world we created in our homes. Some of us forgot our manners or the basic life lessons we learned as children. That doesn't mean we need to avoid the world. We need community. We need to remember not just the ways we are different but the ways we are alike and rejoice in both.

The Light I Bring

SPOKES ON A WHEEL

As humans move from individual isolation to gathering places of connection, possibilities emerge. Much like the way the spokes of a wheel draw energy from the rim to the hub, moving the wheel forward, the closer we come together, the more clearly we see we are not so different from each other. When we engage and connect, we lose our sense of isolation and are re-energized by this connection.

What is it that I bring to this? I don't know. A wheel can miss a spoke or two, but if too many are lost it, it can't move forward. Maybe my gift is to simply show up and add to the light. The biggest lesson I learned from our instructor is the power of consistently showing up, to be a steady, positive spot of light. It doesn't have to be hard.

If nothing else, show up. For me, I know some days I add to the light of the group and sometimes I need the light of others to top my tank, like getting gas at the gas station. Either way it is in gathering as those of the light that the world is made better by this simple act.

This Little Light of Mine

"This little light of mine…"

That song I learned as a child came to mind the other day as I looked out my back window at the heavy rain. For three days it had been rainy and bone-chilling cold.

I was reminded of my first winter in New Orleans. The city is famous for its hot, very humid summers but winters can be hard in their own way. It was a rainy November with the temperatures hovering around 40 degrees for almost a week.

Water doesn't exactly run into the gutters down there because the city sits at or below sea level. It depends on large municipal pumps to pull the surface water into Lake Pontchartrain. If there's more rain than the pumps can handle, then it sits on the ground.

I slopped across the ice-cold water that covered the campus sidewalks. The color of my soaked, fashionable shoes stained my frozen toes. I summed my misery up in one sentence. "And I thought hell would be hot."

My understanding of hell was shaped as a child. It included the devil with a pitchfork chasing children through the dark on Halloween. In my child's mind, I never saw the devil standing in bright light by the seashore, wearing sunglasses or squinting as it looked up at the clear blue sky. The devil was always in the shadows waiting to emerge in surprising ways.

I acknowledge that there is evil on earth, but I've never understood it. I have seen people be cruel and I have borne the brunt of others' misdirected ire. So many times, it seems when people lash out it is at something that they don't want to admit about themselves.

Personally, there is still a mystery in my life anchored in the actions of a certain church leader who came after not just me but others in a nonsensical way that reminds me of certain world leaders.

Do I say that person is evil? No. That's not my place. I can judge that person's actions, but no one but God can judge a heart.

By my desk at the hospital where I worked, I kept a page from an old calendar that said, "Look for the good in others and tell them what you see." Some might call that a platitude, but it's worked pretty well for me.

And when I say my prayers at night, I always include one for world peace. More than some might consider that a platitude, especially in this day and age. I disagree.

If we give up hoping for something better, what kind of life is that? If what we have now is all there is, where is life's joy? If we think that evil will win, then why bother?

I believe in goodness and light. Even at one of the darkest moments in history, my deepest conviction is that light will win. I refuse to give up. My experience has shown me that even the most random hurtful events in my life only win if I let them.

When I say my prayer for peace each night, I imagine the world covered with a thick net similar to the rope nets of a fisherman. The cords of my net are brilliant strings of light like Christmas lights on a tree. The lights sparkle and light the way to a better life.

Yes. These days are challenging, but I ask myself and I ask you, "What can we do to help?" We need to look at ourselves and decide what matters most to us. Then ask another question, "What actions will we commit to?"

For me it starts with prayer and asking for wisdom and strength.

"Please give me strength to do my part however big or little that might be.

Please give me strength to hold my corner of the net of light."

My light?

"…I'm gonna let it shine."

PART X

Fruition
CLOSURE

View From the Back Seat

THE VIEW from the back seat of a car is different from the one behind the wheel. Usually, I'm a solo driver and on the long drives, my hands are on the steering wheel and my focus is on the road ahead. This trip was different, and it wasn't all bad.

There was a death in my husband's family. The cousin who died was a gentle but strong soul who welcomed me into the family decades earlier. Hers and her husband's wedding gift was the first to arrive those many years ago. That welcoming gesture set the tone for years of friendship.

I wanted to go and honor that connection by attending her funeral nine hours away in Mississippi.

I drove to Nashville where I joined my brother-in-law and his wife for the rest of the journey. I was offered the "shotgun" seat of honor, the front passenger seat, and over the course of the hours long trip the three of us shared stories of those who we knew and loved and were no longer with us.

The trip had come together seamlessly. The three of us had clear schedules but more importantly, we had the desire to come together once more as an extended family. We wanted to go through the ritual of standing together at the funeral home as we had for so many who had gone on ahead of us. Our generation shared history and there was a bit of longing for the time when those whose names now on tombstones stood near in full flesh.

"For everything there is a season…"

Our destination was Vicksburg, the town known to the Union Army as "the Gibraltar of the South," for its tenacious Civil War battle. That fight's ghost remains even now and as we rode, I wondered what ghosts might be waiting for me.

My first trip to Vicksburg was in the 1970s when my future husband gave me the tour of his hometown. In our early married years, we showed back up there on a regular basis because part of my husband longed to recreate the days of friendship and connection that town represented to him.

Later we returned to that town as parents and together we raised our sons through high school. It was different, though from the brief sorties of before. The brief early trips were nostalgia filled. Yet everyday life was challenging as we tried to recreate for our sons the childhoods that had been ours.

But real life in a physical world was different from what we had recalled. That past we remembered was in a particular time and place. No matter how we tried, we were attempting to recreate a time and space that was only fully true in our memories. It was much like trying to catch a half-remembered dream that lingers on the edge of consciousness after we've awakened.

Memories. So many memories. Vicksburg was now a part of me too. Would being there again stir those feelings of longing for me?

The funeral went well. We said our good-byes. I saw long ago friends and lots of family. My generation is now a little thicker in the middle and a little more stooped. I stood once again with men with long-legged traits that they shared with my husband. I was glad that we came to honor the connection that had been so important to him. He would have been pleased.

On the trip home I asked to sit in the back seat. I needed to ruminate on that time just spent in the space so important to my husband, my sons and to me. The view from the back was very different and rather than looking at the road ahead I gazed at the tall pines and thick undergrowth whizzing by.

I felt surprisingly detached about that town. This was the first visit where I didn't feel the need to drive by the homes of those long ago gone. I didn't need those physical representations of the memories anymore. It was kind of a relief.

Even when I touched my husband's headstone and thanked him for a beautiful life together, a few tears rolled down my cheek. The knee buckling sobs of previous visits were missing and I found myself not missing the grief that had enveloped me for so long. That too was kind of a relief.

I shifted in my back seat and like the lookout in the crow's nest of an ancient ship I shifted my gaze. My eyes looked forward as I realized the point of the trip.

Closure is good. It's like putting the period at the end of a very long sentence.

I Thought I Knew

A NEW WRITING project drew me to the dusty box of old files in the basement that I had avoided for a very long time.

I am ready. The untouched boxes from our last, incredibly difficult move spoke to me and told me it was time to tend to them. I wasn't happy about the task so only reluctantly did I wipe off the dust and open a half-crumpled box. What stared back at me was a collection of my mother-in-law's art supplies. What? She died a quarter century ago. How many times had we moved that box? I set it aside and decided my great-niece, the artist, could sort out that half-dried treasure.

The next box contained old forgotten kitchen tools. Along the edge were a few grease spattered recipes untouched in way too many years. Here was another useless box moved across country. Those tools can go to someone who cooks.

Then an unmarked box beckoned me. I sighed and fought the urge to ignore it, but its voice was too strong. I opened the box and what greeted me was exactly what I was trying to avoid. Piles of handwritten notes welcomed me to dive back into the past. These notes were part of James' life-long dream. He wrote on that book of his, "River City Ebb and Flow," his whole life. It was through a publisher's deep friendship that James held the first copy in his hands before he died.

I met James in a coffee shop in New Orleans back in 1976. He didn't sit on the stool next to me but on the one next to that. It was as he perused the menu that I heard a voice in my head that encouraged me to speak to him or otherwise I "would miss out on something good."

Whether I heard the voice with my head or my heart, I had a choice. I could ignore it or dismiss it as a rambling thought. Or I could say "yes." With the word "yes" I was acknowledging more than opportunity. I was acknowledging possibility.

Stepping into that possibility brought a full, rich life. James died before our 41st wedding anniversary and in those years, we traveled, moved, raised two sons and stood steady for each other. Now what was supposed to happen? I was fully aware that If I lived as long as my mother did, a full thirty years lay ahead and this time it would be I would be navigating on my own.

It was March right before the third anniversary of James' death that I traveled to Detroit to visit my son and his family. Outside was that end of winter cold and gray but my son's home sent out a lighthouse beam for me to move toward.

The last time I saw the family was in November right after the baby was born. I was still in the fog then. This fog of grief is something that hangs on for a while. It's not dynamic like the fog clouds that spin and slowly moved near the edge of the river as the wind slowly pushes it in one direction of another. This was cold and gray and stagnant.

This fog came on gradually. It probably began setting in around the time of James' initial terminal diagnosis. Slowly over time it grew thicker and darker. In a way it was like my own shroud calling to me. If only I would acknowledge it, it just might set me free.

Some stories stand repeating and this is one.

Clare Biedenharn, DMin, BCC

There in my son's home we were sitting in the kitchen. I forget our topic of discussion, but I felt like I was talking more than usual, and my sentences had more words. I felt sort of animated. Through the course of the conversation, I noticed my son and my daughter-in-law exchanging glances. Then it struck me. I was different even from when I was last there just four months earlier.

I acknowledged what needed to be said. "I noticed your glances. I guess the biggest change for me since I saw you last is that I've decided it's okay to be happy."

They both jumped in with, "Of course it's ok to be happy." What they didn't realized that it was a matter of giving myself permission that was the big hurdle. I was shrouded in fog for years and I could have continued my slumber like Sleeping Beauty for another hundred years. I didn't want that, though. I didn't want to die. I realized finally that I wanted to live.

Once my grief was like dark, thick dust settled around my ankles only to kicked up every so often. Now when I sweep my pile of grief into the dustpan, I can take it outside and toss it to the sky. It glitters in the sunlight and the breeze catches it. Now it is light, not dark. The wind gently carries it away.

My beloved, you know my heart. One day we'll be together again and for that I will be pleased. For now, other tasks are coming my way. I am grateful to finally reach this understanding. This life I have is a gift and I am grateful for what is to come. I *trust* what is to come.

After all, I trusted that wise voice that brought us together decades ago. My hungry ears lean in to hear it better because I know it will show me the way.

I trust it still.

About the Author

Rev Dr Clare Biedenharn, author, speaker, trainer, is a board-certified chaplain with nearly 30 years of chaplaincy experience in industry, critical care and working with organ donor families. She was the first female industrial chaplain in Mississippi, wearing a hard hat and climbing on oil rigs. From there she transitioned to the bedside in the hospital critical care setting which ultimately led to supporting families of organ donors as they faced end- life decisions. Through her years of hands-on experience, she came to embrace the belief that intentional listening is an essential element of every type of communication.

Her lifelong mission is to support stressed out nurses and other healthcare professionals through use of an intentional listening model that she field tested at the hospital in New Orleans. Currently that model guides her work international travel nurses.

The day that Clare was defending her dissertation in Chicago, her husband James was scanned for what was to be terminal cancer. She set aside her work to provide for his care, but James always encouraged her to return to work that she loved. Following his death she did.

Her first book, *Heart to Heart: Spiritual Care through Deep Listening*, detailed the listening study she led at a hospital in New Orleans. Her second book, *Reflect, Reconnect, Restore: Healing from Secondary Grief,* evolved from work with healthcare leadership caught in grief following the COVID-19 lockdown.

Dr Clare continues to contribute to the medical community through research such as the recent article on the healing power of stories based on those posted to the IHI website by frontline workers and their families. Also, she has published multiple times in *Guideposts* magazine following her acceptance to the prestigious Writers Workshop.

Dr Clare served churches as an ordained minister in the United Methodist Church for ten years before embracing fulltime chaplaincy. She is the mother of two adult sons who were each wise enough to marry smart and loving women. Four wonderful grandchildren bless her life.

Further information Dr Clare's listening project is available at -https://YourListeningPartner.com

Also by Clare Biedenharn, DMin, BCC

Bibliography

Biedenharn, C. & Gampetro, P. J., Schultz, C. M. & (2023) Hermeneutic Analysis of International Stories: Lived Experiences During the COVID-19 Pandemic. *American Journal of Qualitative Research, 7* (2), 206-225.

Biedenharn, C (2022). *Reflect, Reconnect, Restore: Healing from Secondary Grief.* A Page Beyond Press.

Biedenharn, C. (2020). *Heart to Heart: Spiritual Care through Deep Listening.* A Page Beyond Press.

Biedenharn, C. (2014). A Study of Critical Care Nurses' Listening Behavior through the Application of the Quaker Listening Model (Dissertation) Garrett Theological Seminary.

Biedenharn, J. (2017) River City Ebb and Flow: Dr. Jas. O'Phelan's Stories from the Wicker Basket under this Fragile Balloon. Canopic Press.

Bolte-Taylor, J. (2009). *My Stroke of Insight: A Brain Scientist's Personal Journey.* Penguin Books.

Gampetro, P. J., Schultz, C. M., & Biedenharn, C. (2023). Hermeneutic Analysis of International Stories: Lived Experiences During the COVID-19 Pandemic. *American Journal of Qualitative Research, 7(2),* 206-225.

Kubler-Ross, E. (1974). *On Death and Dying.* Scribner.

Mate, G. (2011). *When the Body Says No: Exploring the Stress-Disease Connection.* Trade Member Press.

Mullainathan, S., and Shafir, E. (2014). *Scarcity: The New Science of Having Less and How It Defines Our Lives.* Picador Publishing.

Coombs, M., & Nemeck, OMI, F. (1990). *The Spiritual Journey.* Liturgical Press.

Pigott, J., Hargreaves, J., & Power, J. (2016). *Liminal hospital spaces: Corridors to well-being?* The Third International Conference Exploring Multi-Dimensions of Well-Being.

Sanders. C. (2003) *The Complete Poems of Carl Sandberg.* Houghton Mifflin Harcourt.

Skiano. R. (2021). Behind the Screen: A Winner's Guide to Your Next Audition. Ralph Skiano Press.

Van der Kolk, M.D., B. (2005) *The Body Keeps the Score: Brain, Mind and Body in the Healing of Trauma.* Penguin Books

Vedantam, S. (2019). *In the heat of the moment: How intense emotions transforms us.* Hidden Brain [Podcast].

www.ingramcontent.com/pod-product-compliance
Lightning Source LLC
Chambersburg PA
CBHW032042150426

43194CB00006B/393